School Information System and Data-based Decision-making
Schulinformationssysteme und datengestützte Entscheidungsprozesse

Andreas Breiter
Angelina Lange
Emese Stauke
(eds./Hrsg.)

School Information Systems and Data-based Decision-making

Schulinformationssysteme und datengestützte Entscheidungsprozesse

PETER LANG
Frankfurt am Main · Berlin · Bern · Bruxelles · New York · Oxford · Wien

Bibliografische Information der Deutschen Nationalbibliothek
Die Deutsche Nationalbibliothek verzeichnet diese Publikation
in der Deutschen Nationalbibliografie; detaillierte bibliografische
Daten sind im Internet über <http://www.d-nb.de> abrufbar.

ISBN 978-3-631-57030-2
© Peter Lang GmbH
Internationaler Verlag der Wissenschaften
Frankfurt am Main 2008
Alle Rechte vorbehalten.

Das Werk einschließlich aller seiner Teile ist urheberrechtlich geschützt. Jede Verwertung außerhalb der engen Grenzen des Urheberrechtsgesetzes ist ohne Zustimmung des Verlages unzulässig und strafbar. Das gilt insbesondere für Vervielfältigungen, Übersetzungen, Mikroverfilmungen und die Einspeicherung und Verarbeitung in elektronischen Systemen.

www.peterlang.de

Table of Contents

Preface 7

Andreas Breiter:
Integrating School Management Information Systems 11

First Part: Data use in Schools 21

Adrie J. Visscher:
The utilization of school performance feedback systems for
school improvement 23

Cornelia Brunner & Daniel Light:
From Knowledge Management to Data-Driven Instructional
Decision-Making in Schools: The Missing Link 37

Ingmar Hosenfeld et al.:
Projekt VERA: Ergebnisorientierte Unterrichtsentwicklung
durch internetgestützte externe Evaluation? 49

Martin Mechtel:
IT-Unterstützung der Testaufgabenentwicklung am IQB 61

Ian Selwood:
Managing with ICT in Education. 71

Second Part: Large Scale School Management Information Systems 81

Emese Stauke:
Rückmeldesystem zur Kompetenzmessung in Ungarn 83

Pius Bischofberger:
Schulstatistik oder Management Information System? 95

Jeffery Watson:
Defining Data Quality for Decision Support Systems in Education 101

Don Passey:
Data integration and school management systems in the United Kingdom 109

Vainas Brazdeikis:
East European Case: from Data to EMIS 119

Preface

Information management in the context of school administration is a rather new topic in German research and practice of school management. In order to fill the gap and to exchange experience, the State Department of Education (Senator of Education and Science) in Bremen (Senatorin für Bildung und Wissenschaft, SfBW) and the Institute of Information Management Bremen (ifib) have organized an international "Workshop on School Information Systems and Data-Driven Decision-Making" in April 2007 in Bremen. The workshop was divided in two parts: on the first day, national researchers and practitioners discussed current developments in German States (Laender). On the second day, they mixed with international experts from five different countries (United States, United Kingdom, Netherlands, Lithuania and Switzerland).

The following papers span an area from nation-wide or State-wide approaches to implement large-scale databases for data analysis (data warehouses) to research on the actual use of the provided data by teachers to inform classroom-level decisions. The papers provide evidence on activities on all levels of the schools system – from state information system to district data warehouses and to classroom support.

This publication is divided into two parts depending on the scope which is addressed. The first papers provide information about the use of data in individual schools. The second part is composed of different case studies and experiences with large-scale school information systems.

The introductory chapter by *Andreas Breiter* provides us with an overview about the research field and current developments. His integration model emphasizes the importance of interoperability and the role of requirements analysis for a sustainable implementation of user-centered school management information systems (SMIS).

First Part: Data use in Schools
As one of the major researchers in the field, *Adrie Visscher* from the University of Twente (Netherlands) has analyzed the use of performance feedback systems for school improvement. Out of his research, the current focus on accountability is counter-productive for sustainable use.

Cornelia Brunner and *Daniel Light* from EDC's Center for Children and Technology (CCT) in New York explain the missing link which was derived from their empirical research in different U.S. district to implement data-driven decision making.

A very different perspective on the use of test data is offered by *Ingmar Hosenfeld, Ursula Koch, Jana Groß-Ophoff* and *Frank Schertan* from the University of Landau. Being the main research team on the standardized test implementation in elementary schools (VERA, "Vergleichsarbeiten"), they focus on the data use by teachers and the change in classroom management.

In his paper, *Martin Mechtel* points out the current developments at the National Institute for Quality in Education (IQB). The main focus is on the implementation of "task databases" in order to improve the workflow for large-scale data collection in national standardized tests.

Finally for this section of the book *Ian Selwood* from the University of Birmingham tries to bridge the gap between techno-centric approaches and the real value for education reform and change.

Second Part: Large Scale SMIS

Emese Stauke from the University of Bremen starts the first part on country case studies. Her insights on the developments in Hungary highlight the strong link between existing state-wide testing activities, IT support for data analysis and the use by teachers.

A very progressive example of implementing and maintaining a district-wide information system is offered by *Pius Bischofberger* from Kanton Zurich, Switzerland. He describes among others the integration of historical data (back to 1832) and geographic data.

Jeff Watson from the Wisconsin Center of Educational Research (WCER) of the University of Wisconsin at Madison provides us with the large picture on IT-based data warehouses which are used to analyze value-added school reform.

In a second report from the UK *Don Passey* from the University of Lancaster illustrates the development from hand-made singular information systems in schools to large-scale movements for a school interoperability framework.

Perorating the collection of large-scale experiences, *Vainas Brazdeikis* from the Centre of Information Technologies of Education Vilnius in Lithuania describes the introduction process of a nationwide education management system from the vision over the strategy up to the current status and future plans.

Preface

We hope the reader will enjoy this compilation of current research on School Management Information Systems and their technical and organizational integration into the current, grown environment. It should show that there are a lot of open questions to be answered in the next years to provide a good basis for information management and decision making in the currently fast changing education systems.

We are very thankful for the support of the SfBW, especially Dietmar Kirchhoff, who encouraged us to organize this workshop and provided us with a lot of input and contacts.

Bremen, October 2007

Andreas Breiter
Emese Stauke
Angelina Lange

Integrating School Management Information Systems

Andreas Breiter

Information and Communication Technologies in Schools
Information and communication technologies have a massive impact on the way schools work. The major focus of research can be found on the use of digital media in classrooms. There is a large amount of empirical data on how learners can be supported, how teachers can improve their didactical processes and how both, teachers and students, can gain media literacy. There are five core areas in which information and communication technologies are used in school environments:
- As digital media to enrich teaching and learning experiences
- As learning tools to support individual learning processes
- As distribution channels for globally available digital resources for teaching and learning material
- As a topic of teaching and learning processes (critical and reflective use of media)
- As algorithmic machines to be programmed (in informatics / computer science)

In all of theses areas, there is a rich body of research with ambivalent results concerning the impact of information and communication technologies. On the one hand, there is empirical evidence that learning can be more effective – usually measured with standardized tests (e.g. OECD, 2004). Other studies suggest that digital media support individual learning processes if used in enriching authentic classroom settings (e.g. Owston, 2007). On the other hand, we can find empirical studies, which show relatively low impact on measurable competencies but higher impact on skills like media literacy (e.g. Schaumburg, 2003).

These fields and studies can be summarized as the "pedagogical sphere" of the school system. Directly related to it, but often neglected in research, is the "administrative sphere". Any school system has to be planned, organized and controlled. The managerial tasks range from top-level decision-making (usually at the State level) to building-level management for the principal and classroom-level decision-making of the individual teacher. Without overemphasizing the role of administration for teaching and learning processes, schools without school management would not exist. The two spheres are ultimately interconnected and they are interdependent.

With the introduction of information and communication technologies in public administrations, school management has been a target in most countries. In the 1960's and 1970's, the term "Information Resource Management" was coined in U.S. literature (e.g. Synnott & Gruber, 1981). As the theoretical foundations suggested, information will become an important resource for administrative processes. This was extended to a large interdisciplinary research field on information management (Choo, 2002; E. Davenport, 1988; Earl, 1996; Krcmar, 2004), which can be summarized as the way to provide adequate information for a specific target group, on time and in quality. The underlying software systems and IT infrastructure has changed throughout the decades:

- Decision support systems (DSS) in the 1970s
- Management Information Systems (MIS) in the 1980s
- Knowledge Management Systems (KMS) (in the 1990s)
- Date Warehouses (DWH) and Business Intelligence today

The main goal remained to support managerial decisions by highly automated processes. Taking into account the increased significance of "information" as a prime resource in management contexts and its importance for the support of decision-making processes, various approaches to information management were developed in the beginning of the 70's. MIS are based on the assumption that availability of relevant information is a necessary condition for decisions. Simon (1977) suggested three phases of decision-making: intelligence (review the environment, analyze goals, collect data, identify problem, categorize problem, assess ownership and responsibility), design (develop alternative courses of action, analyze potential solutions, create model, test for feasibility, validate results) and choice (acceptability of solution, building normative models). In all three phases information has to be provided and/or searched for in different forms and levels of aggregation. Essentially, management decisions can be understood as information processing where information takes on a strategically important significance for the organization's development (Simon, 1977).

In the beginning of the 1970's, Gorry and Scott Morton (1971) recounted, in an empirical study, that the first MIS failed mainly because it was based on a flawed understanding of managerial work and a fundamental misunderstanding regarding the necessary information (Gorry & Scott Morton, 1971). The predominant perspective at that time, which is still common today among many system developers, is based on a naïve understanding of decision-making processes. It was thought that decisions can be exclusively rationalized and it took some years to understand the "bounded rationality" of decision-makers (Simon 1977). Built on this conception, company-wide projects collected data from every department and sub-department to be stored in a central database, which managers could use to make the "right" decisions. Through extensive case studies Gorry and Scott Morton (1971) showed that only a small portion of the collected data was relevant for decision-making and most of the data was totally worthless for decision-making.

Ackoff (1989) elaborates on the fundamental flawed assumptions that accompanied the development of MIS. The preconceptions underlying the design of early MIS presupposed that the crucial need of management was the availability of all relevant information (Ackoff, 1989). The early designers failed to realize that good management requires the reduction of irrelevant information to focus on relevant information when making a decision. The early MIS systems overloaded decision-makers with extraneous and irrelevant information, which merely complicated their task of selecting out the relevant data. This mistaken assumption was also exacerbated by actual managers who, when asked, in the abstract, would usually request all possible information but then get lost in data overload. It is important to bear in mind, however, that the definition of relevant information is often hard for managers as they usually act with unclear information. Feldman and March (1988), too, doubt that the provision of requested information should be sufficient to make good decisions. Their assumption is that, often, the necessary information only can be identified when the decisions have already been made (Feldman & March, 1988). Even if essential information is already available to the decision-makers it is frequently ignored during the decision-making process.

MIS literature has moved forward to what is called "business intelligence". The underlying assumption remains that enough efficient computers would be able to remove the problems of user-friendly data analysis. The latest approaches, like data warehousing, integrate multiple databases and promise the use special algorithms ("data mining") that will uncover hitherto unknown connections in large-scale databases (see e.g. Laudon & Laudon, 2002; Marakas, 2003). But even these technologically complex systems do not meet the demands of decision-makers who expect more than simple predefined reports. In the end of the 90's the hardware still was not efficient enough to carry out the analyses. Longitudinal analyses were difficult because only limited historical data was available. OLAP ("On-Line Analytical Processing") brought the expectation that now complex, fast, and user-friendly data bank inquiries could be performed.

IT Support for Data-driven Decision-making in Schools
Especially in Germany, there is only little research on the administrative use of ICT in schools. In Breiter and Light (2006) we suggested a three-column model for information systems in schools, which was based on earlier research (Visscher, 1991). This can be refined to the following landscape:

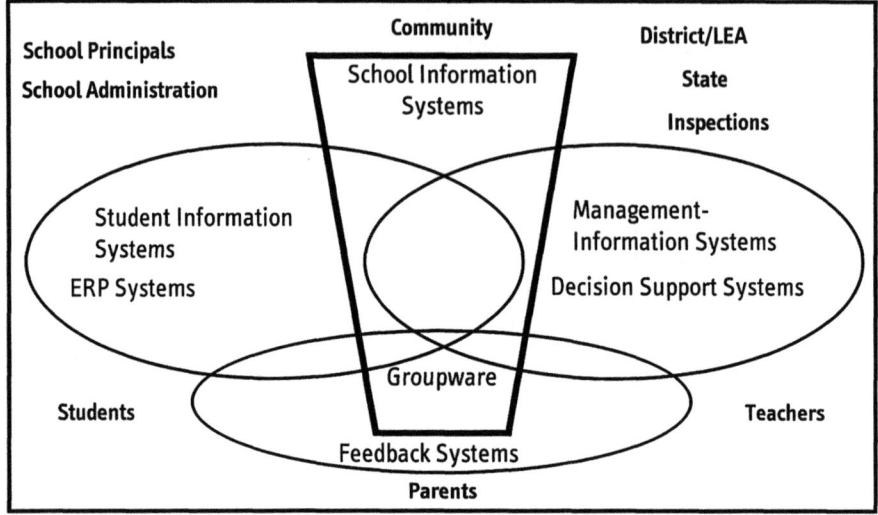

Figure 1: Landscape of School Information Systems

School Information Systems is the general term to describe IT support for external and internal information management:
- Student Information Systems and Enterprise Resource Planning Systems (ERP) span the whole area of basic data – from addresses to scheduling and timetables, to accounting and finance.
- School Management Information System and Decision Support Systems are tailored for building-level decision makers as well as for State Departments of Education for long-term strategic developments and operative controlling.
- Groupware Systems or Computer Support for Collaborative Work (CSCW) help schools to distribute documents internally, to work with shared calendars and to communicate within the school. These can be extended to Wikis or other social software tools.
- Feedback Systems provide data about student performance in combination with context data for classroom level decision-making as well as for parents. Assessment data can be derived from standardized tests, classroom-based assessments (i.e. teacher designed) or from portfolios of student work.

We can learn from the empirical research in MIS that decision-makers at different levels of the school system have different information needs, which first have to be identified and analyzed. In the school system four action levels with specific actor groups can be distinguished that each have different needs of information (see table 1).

Level	Stakeholders	Information needs
Classroom	▪ Teachers ▪ Students	▪ Disaggregated student data ▪ Grades and test scores / portfolios ▪ Tracking of attendance / suspensions
School	▪ Principal ▪ Administrators	▪ Aggregated longitudinal student data (i.e. by class, by subject) ▪ Grades and test scores ▪ Tracking of attendance / suspensions ▪ Aggregated longitudinal administrative data ▪ Coordination of class scheduling ▪ Special education and special programs scheduling ▪ Allocation of human resources ▪ Professional development ▪ Finance and budgeting
District	▪ Superintendent ▪ Administrators	▪ Aggregated longitudinal student data (i.e. by building, by grade) ▪ Aggregated longitudinal administrative data (i.e. by building, by grade) ▪ External data reporting requirements
School Environment	▪ Parents ▪ Local community	▪ Disaggregated student data ▪ Aggregated administrative data

Table 1: Model of levels of information needs in schools (Breiter & Light, 2006)

Today, most data in schools is available in digital form. Research about using test data to support classroom-level decisions or building-level planning to improve learning is just beginning to emerge. In the U.S., the research from different design sites that are piloting educational data-systems are seen in: the Quality School Portfolio (QSP) developed at CRESST (Mitchell & Lee, 1998), and IBM Reinventing Education data projects in Broward County Florida (Spielvogel, 2001). Research on the role of data systems and applications in practice is also being done in San Francisco (Symonds, 2003), in Texas (Stringfield, Wayman, & Yakimowski-Srebnick, 2005) and in Milwaukee (Thorn & Meyer, 2006).

Additionally, there is a body of empirical research on the use of school information systems in other countries, e.g. New Zealand (Nolan, Brown, & Graves, 2001), Netherlands (Visscher & Bloemen, 1999), an examination of experiences with a widely used school information systems in Great Britain (Wild, Smith, & Walker, 2001) and in Hong Kong (Fung & Ledesma, 2001. In Germany, most studies primarily focus on test administration and paper-based feedback mechanisms (for an overview see e.g. Kohler & Schrader, 2004; Weinert, 2001). Nevertheless, most studies mainly focus on administrative data for school management. Less emphasis is given to the role of data for teachers in their instructional decision-making on the classroom-level.

Integrating School Management Information Systems

Usually, integration has a positive connotation as the act of combining something into an integral whole, which should be better than its parts. Integration of ICT as digital media in educational environments can have three dimensions (see also Tearle, 2003): educational (using digital media to increase school quality), organizational (embedding digital media in existing structures and processes), and technical (combining different digital media to support educational and administrative processes). We will concentrate on the last dimension. Reasoning about integrating existing information systems has two contradictory perspectives:

(1) Any approach that wants to be successful has to take into account the individual needs (and fears) of the data owners (privacy) as well as the requirements of the data users (usability). In some cases, these two perspectives do not fit. Most systems are built top-down, gathering as much data as possible and thinking about data use later. Information systems are often flooded with data, offering more data than decision-makers can effectively synthesize and use. As we know from participatory design (e.g. Alexander & Maiden, 2004; Schuler & Namioka, 1993), integrating users into the development process and closely tailoring the tools according to their needs has higher chances to evolve usable software products. Teachers have a wealth of 'tacit knowledge', which needs to be elicited for designing more effective and efficient systems. As largely debated in several approaches to knowledge management (e.g. Davenport & Prusak, 1998; Earl, 2001; Nonaka & Takeuchi, 1995), there is still a lack of systematic analysis of requirements using the hidden expertise of practitioners. Closely related to knowledge management are professional development strategies to support teachers and decision-makers in how to use data. As Visscher, Selwood and others have pointed out (Selwood, Fung, & O'Mahony, 2003; Visscher, 1996), teachers have long experience with standardized testing and curriculum standards, but they do not know how to use information systems to link data to instructional decision-making. Hence, information systems need to be integrated in a socio-cultural environment.

(2) Efficient and effective data use requires up-to-date software systems which are interlinked and allow direct access to all relevant data. Today, most applications in schools and districts are either closed systems or systems that allow access only through proprietary interfaces and data formats. As a consequence, software tools and their data are isolated from one another, data entry is redundant, data quality is unclear, reporting is costly and inefficient, and data is inaccessible to building-level decision makers. From a technological perspective, interoperability of heterogeneous information

systems is a big issue for corporate organizations and large public administrations (EU, 2004). Basically, there are three options (see also Petrides & Guiney, 2002): (a) building-up a large-scale system that includes all existing systems; (b) defining exchange standards between heterogeneous information systems or (c) collecting data in a data warehouse with new interfaces without touching the underlying data infrastructure. Schools in the UK and the US have started to take part in the "Schools Interoperability Framework", which was originated by software industry to provide access between different data systems. In Germany, we are still waiting for such an initiative. This will be very difficult as the 16 Laender have their individual approaches on organizing education.

Conclusions

Building integrated management information systems in schools is ultimately connected with developing these systems with schools. Research in human-centered design has shown that participatory approaches are more likely to produce information systems with high user acceptance. Data-driven decision-making will be an important task for school administrators and teachers in the future; and this will be done with management information systems. Our research suggests that the process for designing integrated school management information systems has to be turned upside down from decision-making to data selection. Instead of starting with the available data, designers need to start from the source of the data – the students and their learning needs. The design needs to start from the information needs for decision support of different stakeholders, which are defined by their different relationships to the students. From that premise, MIS designers should then consider which presentation formats and representations of data are relevant to meet those different needs. From this knowledge, an information system can then be built that houses the decision-relevant data that will help educators more effectively guide the students' learning. From a socio-technical perspective, integrating these systems to increase user acceptance will be a major endeavor.

References:

Ackoff, R. L. (1989). From Data to Wisdom. Journal of Applied Systems Analysis, 16, 3-9.
Alexander, I. F., & Maiden, N. (Eds.). (2004). Scenarios, Stories, Use Cases. Through the Systems Development Life-Cycle. New York: Wiley.
Breiter, A., & Light, D. (2006). Data for School Improvement: Factors for designing effective information systems to support decision-making in schools. IEEE Educational Technology & Society, 9(3), 206-217.
Choo, C. W. (2002). Information Management for an Intelligent Organization: The Art of Environmental Scanning. 3rd Edition. Medford, NJ: Information Today.

Davenport, E. (1988). Information management: a perspective. International Journal of Information Management, 8, 255-263.
Davenport, T. H., & Prusak, L. (1998). Working Knowledge. How Organizations Manage what they Know. Boston: Harvard Business School Press.
Earl, M. J. (2001). Knowledge Management Strategies: Towards a Taxonomy. Journal of Management Information Systems, 18(1), 215-233.
Earl, M. J. (Ed.). (1996). Information Management: The Organizational Dimension. Oxford: Oxford University Press.
EU. (2004). European Interoperability Framework for Pan-european eGovernment Services. Luxembourg: European Communities.
Feldman, M. S., & March, J. G. (1988). Information in Organizations as Signal and Symbol. In J. G. March (Ed.), Decision and Organizations (pp. 409-428). Oxford: Basil Blackwell.
Fung, A. C. W., & Ledesma, J. (2001). SAMS in Hong Kong Schools: A Centrally Developed SIS for Primary and Secondary Schools. In A. J. Visscher, P. Wild & A. C. W. Fung (Eds.), Information Technology in Educational Management. Synthesis of Experience, Research and Future Perspectives on Computer-Assisted School Information Systems (pp. 39-53). Heidelberg: Springer.
Gorry, G. A., & Scott Morton, M. S. (1971). A Framework for Management Information Systems. Sloan Management Review, 13(1), 55-70.
Kohler, B., & Schrader, F.-W. (Eds.). (2004). Ergebnisrückmeldung und Rezeption. Von der externen Evaluation zur Entwicklung von Schule und Unterricht. Themenheft Empirische Pädagogik, 18 (1). Landau: Verlag Empirische Pädagogik.
Krcmar, H. (2004). Information Management (1. Aufl ed.). Berlin: Springer-Verlag GmbH & Co. KG.
Laudon, K., & Laudon, J. P. (2002). Management information systems: managing the digital firm, 7th edition. Englewood Cliffs, NJ: Prentice-Hall.
Marakas, G. M. (2003). Modern Data Warehousing, Mining, and Visualization. Core Concepts. Upper Saddle River, NJ: Pearson.
Mitchell, D., & Lee, J. (1998). Quality school portfolio: Reporting on school goals and student achievement. Paper presented at the CRESST Conference, Los Angeles, CA.
Nolan, C. J. P., Brown, M. A., & Graves, B. (2001). MUSAC in New Zealand: From Grass Roots to System-Wide in a Decade. In A. J. Visscher, P. Wild & A. C. W. Fung (Eds.), Information Technology in Educational Management. Synthesis of Experience, Research and Future Perspectives on Computer-Assisted School Information Systems (pp. 55-75). Heidelberg: Springer.
Nonaka, I., & Takeuchi, H. (1995). The Knowledge Creating Company. Oxford: Oxford University Press.
OECD. (2004). Learning for Tomorrow's World – First Results from PISA 2003. Paris: OECD - Centre for Educational Research and Innovations.
Owston, R. (2007). Contextual factors that sustain innovative pedagogical practice using technology: an international study Journal of Educational Change, 8, 61-77.
Petrides, L. A., & Guiney, S. Z. (2002). Knowledge Management for School Leaders: An Ecological Framework for Thinking Schools. Teachers College Record, 104(8), 1702-1717.
Schaumburg, H. (2003). Konstruktivistischer Unterricht mit Laptops? Eine Fallstudie zum Einfluss mobiler Computer auf die Methodik des Unterrichts. Unpublished Diss., Freie Universität Berlin, Berlin.

Schuler, D., & Namioka, A. (Eds.). (1993). Participatory Design. Principles and practices. Hillsdale, NJ: Lawrence Erlbaum.

Selwood, I., Fung, A. C. W., & O'Mahony, C. D. (Eds.). (2003). Management of Education in the Information Age: The Role of ICT, IFIP TC3/WG3.7 Fifth Working Conference on Information Technology in Educational Management (ITEM 2002), August 18-22, 2002, Helsinki, Finland. Norwall, MA: Kluwer.

Simon, H. A. (1977). The New Science of Management Decisions, rev. ed. Englewood Cliffs, NJ: Prentice-Hall.

Spielvogel, B. (2001). IBM Reinventing Education: Research Summary and Perspective. New York: EDC/Center for Children and Technology.

Stringfield, S., Wayman, J. C., & Yakimowski-Srebnick, M. E. (2005). Scaling Up Data Use in Classrooms, Schools, and Districts. In C. Dede, J. P. Honan & L. C. Peters (Eds.), Scaling Up Success: Lessons Learned from Technology-Based Educational Improvement (pp. 133-152). San Francisco, CA: Jossey-Bass.

Symonds, K. W. (2003). After the Test: How Schools are Using Data to Close the Achievement Gap. San Francisco, CA: Bay Area School Reform Collaborative.

Synnott, W. R., & Gruber, W. H. (1981). Information resource management: opportunities and strategies for the 1980s. New York: Wiley.

Tearle, P. (2003). ICT implementation: what makes the difference? British Journal of Educational Technology, 34(5), 567-583.

Thorn, C. A., & Meyer, R. H. (2006). Longitudinal Data Systems to Support Data-Informed Decision Making: A Tri-State Partnership Between Michigan, Minnesota, and Wisconsin Madison, WI: Wisconsin Center for Education Research, University of Wisconsin.

Visscher, A. J. (1991). School administrative computing: A framework for analysis. Journal of Research on Computing in Education, 24(1), 1-19.

Visscher, A. J. (1996). The implications of how staff handle information for the usage of school information systems. International Journal of Educational Research, 25(4), 323-334.

Visscher, A. J., & Bloemen, P. P. M. (1999). Evaluation of the Use of Computer-Assisted Management Information Systems in Dutch Schools. Journal of Research on Computing in Education, 32(1), 172-188.

Weinert, F. E. (Ed.). (2001). Leistungsmessung in Schulen. Weinheim: Beltz.

Wild, P., Smith, D., & Walker, J. (2001). Has a Decade of Computerization Made a Difference in School Management. In C. J. P. Nolan, A. C. W. Fung & M. A. Brown (Eds.), Pathways to Institutional Improvement with Information Technology in Educational Management. IFIP TC3/WG3.7 Fourth Working Conference on Information Technology in Educational Management (ITEM 2000), July 27-31, Auckland, New Zealand (pp. 99-120). Norwell, MA: Kluwer.

First Part: Data use in Schools

The utilization of school performance feedback systems for school improvement

Adrie J. Visscher

Introduction
Internationally seen, there is an increasing trend to feed back information to schools and teachers on their performance. School improvement is often the main objective, however, accountability and the promotion of parental/student school choice also plays a role.

The features of 'school performance feedback systems' (SPFSs) will be analysed just as the factors that have contributed to their international growth. Thereafter, the characteristics of the Dutch school performance feedback system ZEBO will be presented briefly, followed by the presentation of a framework including the factors assumed to influence the utilisation of SPFS-information and its effects.

In the final section some reflections are presented on why schools like to buy SPFSs and how likely it is that the implementation of these systems will lead to better functioning schools.

The nature of school performance feedback systems
School performance feedback systems are defined here as information systems external to schools that provide them with confidential information on their performance and functioning as a basis for school self-evaluation. Such systems have become widespread in education in many parts of the world. They share a goal of seeking to maintain and improve the quality of schools, and arise out of a belief in the power of feedback to learn, and to produce change, often accompanied by a sense of disillusionment at the lack of impact of other models of school improvement.

This definition excludes informal, self-generated feedback and separates SPFSs from systems of *public* school performance accountability and for the support of school choice, which have rather different aims and contents.

The content of the information on the school's *performance or functioning* must be taken broadly. 'School performance' here is likely to mean some kind of contextualised measure for fair comparison, adjusted to take account of factors beyond the control of the school ('value added'). 'Performance' may also include absolute performance measures and may equally relate to non-academic outcomes of schooling (e.g. behavioural and affective). Information on the '*func-*

tioning' of schools relates to organisational and school process measures like the resources spent, the subject matter taught, the instructional methods used, and the nature of school leadership etc.

That the feedback should provide a basis for self-evaluation implies that the feedback should not simply be used for self-assessment, but that once such judgements have been made, they ideally lead to some kind of action, e.g. the closer investigation where and why the schools under-performs, and the development of a school improvement policy.

Reasons for school performance feedback systems
A number of factors seem to have contributed to the growth of formal school performance feedback systems in many countries over the last twenty or so years.

In many western countries in the 1980s and 90s the rise of a political climate of public sector accountability can be observed. The pressure to evaluate and report on the performance of publicly funded educational institutions did not really lead to SPFSs, however, helped to create a climate in which school performance feedback is seen as more salient than previously.

Related to the accountability trend is the trend towards decentralisation in the administration of educational systems. As a result schools are more likely to seek information they can utilise for school quality control, i.e. some sort of SPFS.

There is moreover some evidence (e.g. Murdoch & Coe, 1997) that in some countries schools' perceptions of the unfairness of the public judgements of their effectiveness (cf. Visscher, 2001, for an overview of the drawbacks of public school performance indicators) were a factor in their choice to implement a confidential value added school monitoring system. The published school performance information included average raw achievement of a school's students which did not adjust for relevant features of the student intake (e.g. achievement levels of a school's intake). Schools wanted more accurate and fairer data on their own performance – among other things, to be sure about their performance and about whether improvement was really needed or not.

Next, the progress made in research in the twin fields of school effectiveness and school improvement. The former line of research has resulted in a knowledge base (Scheerens & Bosker, 1997) that can be utilised in developing systems to monitor the quality of schools (e.g. the ZEBO feedback system which will be described below).

Research on school improvement may have influenced the development of SPFSs too, as scientific activity there showed that educational change initiatives imposed upon schools were often not very successful. Innovation and success are considered much more probable if schools themselves are convinced that something needs to be changed ('ownership'). Receiving information on how your school is doing in comparison with similar schools may be a powerful way to make you aware and determined that something needs to be changed in your organisation.

Dalin (1998), McLaughlin (1998) and Miles (1998) stress the local variability of schools, implying that general, centrally developed policies and reform strategies will not lead to educational change in all schools. Schools are considered to differ so much with respect to their performance levels (and the underlying reasons for them), their innovation capacities and contextual characteristics, that change efforts should take much more account of what is called the 'power of site or place'. Smith (1998) goes a step further. He states that as practitioners know their educational practice best they should state the goals and changes to be worked on and, after extensive training, try to accomplish those. Adaptation to the user-context can then be achieved. A SPFS may a valuable tool within this perspective on school improvement, providing timely, high-quality information on how a school 'is doing' as a basis for practitioner-led improvement actions. That may help practitioners in finding problems in their schools as well as in solving them, before it is too late. An important additional effect may be that practitioners gain a better insight into how their school works (enlightenment) and which interventions work best in their situation.

Related to the pessimism of the school improvement authors is the view of Glass (1979) who regards 'education' as a very complex, highly uncertain and unpredictable system on which we possess only incomplete knowledge. We should not try to find eternal truths about which of several things works well in particular circumstances, as a basis for planning and manipulating education at a large distance from the teaching-learning process in schools. What should be done is the diligent monitoring of the system while the services are highly decentralised, the actors are flexible, and can choose from options what they consider best instead of precisely implementing a universal approach that has been developed somewhere at a higher level.

The increase in feeding back information to schools has also been influenced by the development of multi-level and value-added data-analysis models which enable the computation of more reliable and valid information on school functioning. The availability of computerised systems for information processing has made a significant contribution to the logistics of school performance feedback (cf. Visscher, Wild & Fung, 2001).

Last but not least, research results indicate that feedback can be beneficial to future performance. The most comprehensive synthesis of research on feedback effects is Kluger and DeNisi's (1996) meta-analysis. Overall, they found an effect size of 0.41 (0.38 after various exclusions), which they interpret as "suggesting that, on average, feedback intervention has a moderate positive effect on performance" (p. 258). However, the wide range of effects found suggested that various features of the feedback, the task to be performed, or its context were significant moderators of the effect. In other words, we should attempt to clarify under what conditions feedback can optimally enhance performance.

An example: the Dutch ZEBO school performance feedback system
ZEBO is an instrument for primary education of which the development took five years. Thirteen school and classroom process variables (for example, the extent of educational leadership, the achievement orientation of teachers, the way student performance is evaluated, students' time on task, the classroom climate) that had been found in school effectiveness research as correlates of high student performance were selected for the development of ZEBO (Scheerens & Bosker, 1997). In other words, for each of these variables a scale has been developed to measure the variable and to feed back information on this variable in terms of how the school is doing in comparison with the average Dutch primary school.

After two pilots (in 1997 and 1998), a final field test took place in 1999 in a representative sample of 123 schools in the Netherlands. In 2002, the final market version of ZEBO was released in a computerized form. This format allows schools to use ZEBO whenever they need the information, and they can obtain feedback immediately.

The process variables are measured by means of questionnaires for school management, for teachers and for grade 3-8 pupils. After completing the questionnaires in the schools, schools can generate two kinds of feedback:
- *A school report*: One can download graphic and written representations of the results of the school under study in comparison with schools from a national sample on each scale in the school report. Furthermore, the scores of the teachers are compared to the school management scores.
- *A classroom report*: This report is based on information from the pupil and teacher questionnaires. The results from the students of the school in a certain grade are compared to the results of students in the national sample from

that same grade. The responses of the students are also compared to the responses of the teachers.

The factors that matter for the successful implementation of SPFSs
Figure 1 below presents a model depicting the assumed relationships between four groups of factors (Blocks A - D) on the one hand, and the use (Block E) and impact (Block F) of SPFSs on the other. The model is based on a review of the relevant literature (Visscher and Coe, 2002).

The Figure shows that the nature and intensity of SPFS use is supposed to be influenced by the SPFS features, which result from its design process. The nature of the implementation process and the characteristics of schools are also supposed to influence SPFS use. The implementation process can promote SPFS use directly (e.g. by supporting schools in accomplishing the innovation), or indirectly (e.g. via training school staff in the required SPFS skills). Finally, the degree of SPFS use, and the way in which it is used, is expected to lead to intended and unintended effects.

It is important to stress that Figure 1 is meant to clarify which factors influence SPFS use and the resultant effects (so Blocks E and F are crucial). In other words, the Figure neither shows how all factors contribute to the effects in Block F nor how other blocks in the Figure are related. If the latter would have been the case, arrows between other blocks could also have been drawn.

Figure 1 also indicates that the school environment plays a role. For example, the extent to which the school board, district and the community play an active role in running schools and demand high school quality may influence to what degree schools use a SPFS to improve performance. If the quality of school functioning is a hot issue, for instance shown by published league tables and 'punishments' for under-performing schools, then schools may be more inclined to improve than when external quality control is only weak, and parents are unable to choose the school of their choice. The educational system can also play a more supporting role by providing schools with the resources required for change and improvement.

Each of the Blocks in Figure 1 will now be discussed more in detail. It is however impossible to provide much detail here on the reasons for selecting each framework factor. For more details on the backgrounds of the factors the reader can refer to Visscher & Coe, chapter 3 (2002).

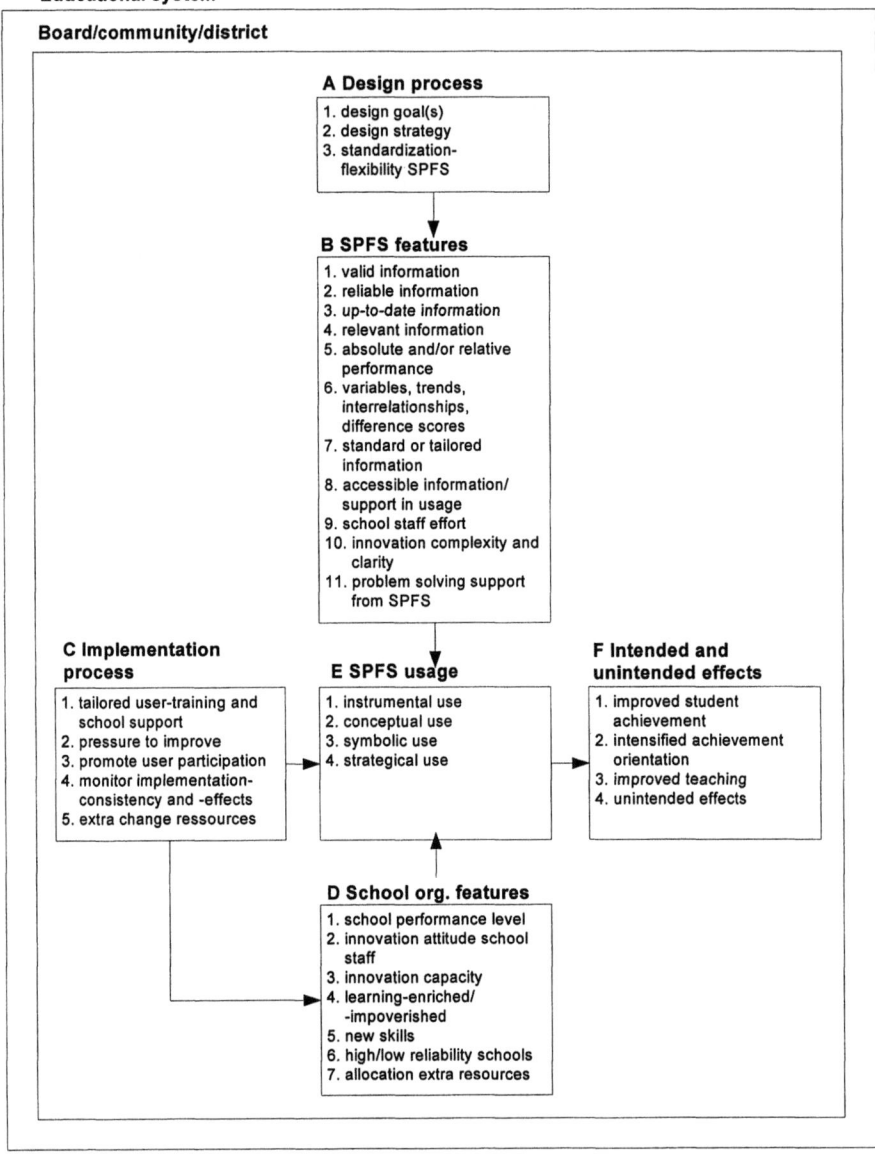

Figure 1: The relationships between the factors influencing SPFS use and effects

Block A: The design process
The process of designing a SPFS can differ in three respects.
1. The goal(s) of designing a SPFS
   Although *school improvement* is the central goal for designing SPFSs some SPFS designers may want to design systems that also serve *accountability*, and the *support of parental school choice*. Each of the three goals requires its own set of performance indicators. Whitford and Jones (1998) state that for school improvement the feedback information should be as detailed as the complexity of schooling. SPFS-designers should be well aware which goal(s) they aim to serve.
2. Design strategies
   Maslowski and Visscher (1999) make a distinction between several design approaches and by that point to aspects of design strategies with implications for our framework:
   - how the problem analysis is carried out, and how objectives and means are formulated in SPFS design;
   - the extent to which SPFS prototypes are developed and evaluated (formative evaluation is of great importance for design optimisation);
   - the degree to which stakeholders communicate with each other and influence decisions on the desired SPFS. If practitioners have more of a say, they may develop ownership, take its findings seriously and make more effort to apply the results (cf. Huberman, 1987; Weiss, 1998);
   - the creative, non-linear side of SPFS design activities.
3. The standardisation - flexibility problem
   Ideally, a SPFS is so flexible that it satisfies requirements uniform to all schools as well as varying information needs among schools. In practice it will be hard to fulfil both goals completely, implying that a compromise between both is usually the most feasible.

Block B: SPFS features
SPFSs can differ in the extent to which:
1. the information it feeds back to schools is *valid,* e.g. value-added data versus raw data, based on multi-level analysis, or aggregated data and the extent to which SPFS data *cover school quality* (e.g. indicators on the performance of the overall school, school divisions, departments, and teachers). Fitz-Gibbon (2002) provides a typology of indicators that can support school improvement;
2. information is *reliable*;
3. information is *up-to-date*: "Timeliness is a useful feature of a report dedicated to utility" (Weiss, 1998);
4. data is *relevant* for practitioners, fits with their needs and reduces their uncertainty;

5. SPFS data indicates both *relative* and *absolute* school performance;
6. data shows values for such *factors* as *trends* over time, *relationships* between data and *differences* between *scores* measured at two or more instances (the latter for example to evaluate the effect of school policy);
7. the SPFS provides *standard* information, and allows in-depth analysis and *tailored* information for users;
8. data is presented in an *accessible* and appealing manner (e.g. quantitatively, graphically) and users are supported in *using* performance *data correctly,* e.g. the correct interpretation of value-added data;
9. the SPFS *requires* the investment of *time and effort* from school staff as a result of data collection and feedback;
10. innovation is *complex* yet *clear*, i.e. the difficulty of the required change and the success of accomplishing it for those who need to make the change.
11. the SPFS provides *user-support in problem-solving* (e.g. via a manual, computer-aided help or help line).

In Block B the importance of sophisticated SPFSs 'spitting out' high quality information is stressed. In Blocks C and D other critical success factors are stressed since SPFS quality is a necessary but insufficient precondition for the use and intended effects of SPFS. Features of schools and the change process itself are strongly related to positive outcomes of school improvement efforts (McLaughlin, 1990).

Block C: Implementation process features
Based on our review of the educational innovation literature the following implementation process features are considered relevant for successfully introducing SPFSs into schools:
1. A lengthy, intensive tailored *reform strategy* and *support*, e.g. assisting in school diagnosis, designing school change policies at class and school level. External change facilitators combed with information exchange via school networks: good examples can fulfil an important role here. The extent, method and content of *user-training* is very important: clarification of innovation goals and means, motivating users for innovation, developing new organisational roles, values, information processing and school improvement skills.
2. The *pressure* to improve via external targets and control, competition between schools and incentives.
3. The encouragement of *user participation* and ownership in implementation.
4. Monitoring the *consistency* of *implementing* SPFSs and SPFS based school innovations within schools as well as the *effects* of SPFS implementation on classrooms and student achievement. Often the implementation process needs to be adapted to the local conditions.

The utilization of school performance feedback systems 31

5. The provision of *extra innovation resources* e.g. for releasing school staff from routine work.

Block D: School organisational features
The following school organisational features of schools are considered important for using a SPFS:
1. The *level of performance* of schools: relatively low levels combined with the pressure strategy may motivate schools more to try to improve performance by using a SPFS.
2. The *innovation attitude* of school staff: receptive or not.
3. The *innovation capacity*: being aware of the school's performance level, structure, culture, problems and the capacity to evaluate, to design reform goals and means, interventions at school and classroom level, experimenting, evaluating, adaptations and improving.
4. The degree to which schools promote *organisational learning*: encouragement and support via shared responsibilities for school goals/outcomes, collaborative work structures, and exchange of information, experimentation and innovation.
5. *New skills*: interpretation of SPFS output.
6. *High/low reliability* schools: the degree to which classroom and other school activities are co-ordinated.
7. Allocation of *school resources* to innovation activities.

Block E: SPFS use
What does SPFS use actually encompass? One element of use concerns the analysis and interpretation of the information received. This may not always be easy as some of the outcomes are the product of the use of complex statistical techniques. Their correct interpretation requires some knowledge of statistical concepts like value-added scores, correlations, and confidence intervals. Ideally, users would have been trained in this respect.

Another aspect of SPFS use concerns the utilisation of the information schools receive for improving their functioning, i.e. deciding to act to improve, and acting on it as much as possible. In the evaluation literature a distinction is made between three types of utilisation (Rossi & Freeman, 1993):
1. *direct or instrumental*: the decision-maker analyses the information before taking a decision, and bases decisions and actions on this;
2. *conceptual*: less visible but also important is the extent to which the evaluative information influences the thinking of decision-makers and as such may have an impact on their actions;

3. *convincing (symbolic)*: this type of use concerns using information in support of someone's own viewpoints in a discussion with others. Information is then used selectively to legitimise an opinion already held.
4. Visscher (2001) refers to Smith (1995) who presents a profound analysis of the unintended, *strategical* consequences of publishing performance data on public sector institutions. Translated to schools one can for example think of the following strategic actions of schools:
   - concentrating on those students where most 'profit' can be gained;
   - selective student admissions;
   - removing 'difficult' students;
   - teaching to the test and by that concentrating on the indicators to the exclusion of other qualifications;
   - consciously depressing baseline test scores to obtain high value-added scores.

Block F: The intended and unintended effects
In our view the ultimate goal of introducing SPFSs should be *improving school performance*, i.e. higher, value-added school performance scores. Proving this type of progress unequivocally will probably take a long time. As long as this goal has not been accomplished it will be interesting to investigate to what degree some important prerequisites for improved school performance can be observed like:
1. a stronger *orientation* of school staff to *high student achievement*;
2. *improved teaching*;
3. changes in school organisational processes and structures because the use of SPFS output presupposes staff co-operation, communication and leadership.
4. However, because of the potential strategical use of performance indicators (Smith, 1995) it is good to check for negative, *unintended effects* of introducing SPFSs.

Drawing up the balance sheet
The fact that thousands of schools around the world want these systems – and are even willing to pay for the support the SPFSs can offer – is rare for the outcomes of educational research and shows that school feedback systems are not just another result of academic, ivory-tower work with little value for the practice of education. That SPFSs are practical thriving entities that are meeting a genuine need in many schools is probably due to the fact that teachers and school managers work in quite uncertain contexts.

Teachers have to manage uncertainty. The goals they have to achieve are often ambiguous and the features of (the input of) student groups differ. Questioning the subject content and teaching methods in a specific teaching situation, as well as the effects of an instructional approach, causes additional uncertainty (McPherson, Crowson & Pitner, 1986; Vilsteren & Visscher, 1987). Since during each lesson period about 200 situational changes occur (Brophy & Good, 1974), teachers do not have time to reflect much on what happens in the classroom and on their own role. Their primary goal is to solve the short-term problem of how to attract the attention of students and how to promote their efforts. To teach is to a large extent 'to improvise well'; judging intuitively what should be done in a specific situation and using heuristics and 'tricks' that have been often proved 'to work'. As a consequence school staff appreciate independent, objective benchmarks on their performance comparing them with other schools that work under similar conditions.

There seems to be a general idea that the process of SPFS development consists of creating something that is believed to be good for schools and, therefore, if introduced properly will be used and will improve the quality of school functioning. SPFS developers in general have not analysed thoroughly what SPFS use presupposes in terms of the change in attitudes and skills of school staff. Enormous resources are invested to accomplish high quality SPFSs. However, the extent of systematic check on how schools deal with the result of all that developmental work appears to be very small.

An exception to this is the study carried out by Schildkamp (2007) who studied to what extent Dutch schools use the ZEBO school performance feedback system, which factors from Figure 1 promoted the introduction of ZEBO, and which effects the use of ZEBO has on student achievement levels and on preconditions for student achievement. ZEBO after a period of 4 years had not led to higher student achievement levels.

An interesting question is of course why this is the case. An important reason may be that the schools that were studied have not been able to grow to levels of ZEBO use that are high enough to have an impact on student achievement. The findings showed that most schools find it difficult to develop the instrumental and conceptual use of ZEBO on their own. It would therefore be interesting to develop strategies for training and supporting schools in the use of ZEBO, and to investigate the effects of these forms of support on levels of ZEBO use, and on student achievement.

Even when schools will use the ZEBO output intensively they probably will not just straightaway be able to improve the functioning of the school in such a way that students learn more. Although this is the idea underlying self-evaluation instruments it may not be that easy to accomplish. Improvement requires a solid analysis of causes of underperformance, taking suitable measures to address these causes, and, last but not least, the school wide implementation of these measures. The average school may not have the required skills for this.

Ehren (2006) found for example also that schools find it very difficult to use the feedback they receive on their functioning from school inspectors as a basis for implementing complex improvement actions. The only improvements the schools accomplished were of a very simple kind (e.g. changing a rule for students). For this reason it may also be necessary to support schools in this respect, to let them gradually develop these skills more. Promising is that the findings showed a gradual growth in the effects of ZEBO use on those school process characteristics which have been shown to be associated with relatively high pupil achievement levels. Several schools used the ZEBO output intensively and in these schools some effects on important prerequisites for school improvement were found. ZEBO use in these schools had a positive impact on consultation, dialogue and reflection. Furthermore, principals and teachers reported an increase in the achievement orientation of staff, more adaptive education, an improved functioning of the principal, and an increase in professional development activities. Some teachers also indicated that they improved their didactic behavior as a result of ZEBO use. The use of ZEBO in general, had no unintended, negative effects.

The development of school self-evaluation instruments receives much attention around the globe, however much is still unknown about the effects of the use of school self-evaluation instruments, and the mechanisms that matter here. The challenge is therefore to investigate how schools can grow to higher levels of use of SPFSs, and how they may benefit more fully in terms of improving the school process characteristics and student performance.

References:

Brophy, J. & Good, T. (1974). Teacher-pupil relationships. New York: Holt, Rinehart & Winston.
Dalin, P. (1998). Developing the twenty-first century school, a challenge to reformers. In Hargreaves, A., Lieberman, A., Fullan, M. & Hopkins, D. (Eds.). International Handbook of Educational Change (vol. 5, pp. 1059-1073). Dordrecht/Boston/London: Kluwer Academic Publishers.
Ehren, M.C.M. (2007). Toezicht en schoolverbetering. [Supervision and school improvement]. Doctoral dissertation. Delft: Eburon.
Fitz-Gibbon, C.T. (2002). A typology of Indicators. In: Visscher, A.J. & Coe, R. (Eds.) (forthcoming). School improvement through performance feedback. Lisse/Abingdon/Exton/Tokyo: Swets and Zeitlinger.
Glass, G.V. (1979). Policy for the Unpredictable (Uncertainty Research and Policy). Educational Researcher, 8(9), 12-14.

Huberman, M. (1987). Steps towards an integrated model of research utilization. Knowledge: Creation, Diffusion, Utilization, vol. 8(4), 586-611.

Kluger, A.N., & DeNisi, A. (1996). The effects of Feedback Interventions on performance: a historical review, a meta-analysis, and a preliminary Feedback Intervention Theory. Psychological Bulletin, 119, 2, 254-284.

Maslowski, R., & Visscher, A.J. (1999). The potential of formative evaluation in program design models. In van den Akker, J., Branch, R.M., Gustafson, K., Nieveen, N. & Plomp, T. (Eds.). Design Methodology and Development Research in Education and Training. Dordrecht: Kluwer Academic Publishers.

McLaughlin, M.W. (1998). Listening and learning from the field: tales of policy implementation and situated practice. In Hargreaves, A., Lieberman, A., Fullan, M. & Hopkins, D. (Eds.). International Handbook of Educational Change (vol. 5, pp. 70-84). Dordrecht/Boston/London: Kluwer Academic Publishers.

McLaughlin, M.W. (1990). The Rand change agent study revisited; macro perspectives and micro realities, Educational Researcher, 19 (9), 11-16.

McPherson, R.B., Crowson, R., & Pitner, N.J. (1986). Managing Uncertainty: administrative theory and practice in education. Columbus: C.E. Merril Publishing Company.

Miles, M.B. (1998). Finding Keys to School Change: A 40-year Odyssey. In Hargreaves, A. Lieberman, A. Fullan, M. & Hopkins, D. (Eds.). International Handbook of Educational Change (vol. 5, pp. 37-39). Dordrecht/Boston/London: Kluwer Academic Publishers.

Murdoch, K. & Coe, R. (1997). Working with ALIS: a study of how schools and colleges are using a value added and attitude indicator system. Durham: School of Education, University of Durham, United Kingdom.

Rossi, P.H., & Freeman, H.E. (1993). Evaluation; a systematic approach. Newbury Park/London/New Delhi: Sage.

Scheerens, J. & Bosker, R.J. (1997). The foundations of educational effectiveness. Oxford: Elsevier Science Ltd.

Schildkamp, K. (2007). The utilisation of a self-evaluation instrument for primary education. Doctoral dissertation. Enschede: Print Partners Ipskamp.

Smith, P. (1995). On the Unintended Consequences of Publishing Performance Data in the Public Sector. International Journal of Public Administration, 18 (2&3), 277 -310.

Smith, L.M. (1998). A kind of educational idealism: integrating realism and reform. In HargreavesA., Lieberman, A., Fullan, M. & Hopkins, D. (Eds.). International Handbook of Educational Change (vol. 5, pp.100-120). Dordrecht/Boston/ London: Kluwer Academic Publishers.

Van Vilsteren, C.A. & Visscher, A.J. (1987). Schoolwerkplanning: mogelijk in schoolorganisaties? [School work planning: possible in school organisations?] In Creemers, B., Giesbers, J., van Vilsteren, C. & van der Perre, C. (Eds.). Handboek Schoolorganisatie en onderwijsmanagement (pp. 6120-6124). Alphen aan den Rijn: Samson.

Visscher, A.J. (2001). Public School Performance Indicators: problems and recommendations. Studies in Educational Evaluation, 27(3), 199-214.

Visscher, A.J. & Coe, R. (2002). Drawing up the balance sheet for school performance feedback systems. In Visscher, A.J. & Coe, R. (Eds.) (forthcoming). School improvement through performance feedback. Lisse/Abingdon/Exton/Tokyo: Swets and Zeitlinger.

Visscher, A.J., Wild, P., & Fung, A. (Eds.). (2001). Information Technology in Educational Management; synthesis of experience, research and future perspectives on computer-assisted school information systems. Dordrecht/Boston/London: Kluwer Academic Publishers.

Weiss, C.H. (1998). Improving the use of evaluations: whose job is it anyway? In Reynolds, A.J. & Walberg, H.J. (Eds.). *Advances in Educational Productivity*, volume 7, pp. 263-276. Greenwich/London: JAI Press.

Whitford, B.L. & Jones, K. (1998). Assessment and accountability in Kentucky: how high stakes affects teaching and learning. In Hargreaves, A., Lieberman, A., Fullan, M. & Hopkins, D. (Eds.). International Handbook of Educational Change (vol. 5, pp. 1163-1178). Dordrecht/ Boston/London: Kluwer Academic Publishers.

From Knowledge Management to Data-Driven Instructional Decision-Making in Schools: The Missing Link

Cornelia Brunner and Daniel Light

Data and Decisions

This presentation is based on a study funded by the National Science Foundation of the US (REC# 03356653) in which we were trying to define a model of how different technologies can support data-driven decision-making for instructional decisions in the classroom as well as at the school and district levels. The study combined a model for evaluating the affordances of three different technological supports, an online test reporting system, data warehouses, and diagnostic assessments delivered via handheld computers. Borrowing from Russell Ackoff's (1989) work in the field of organization and management theory, we adapted a simplified version of his conceptual framework that links data, information, and knowledge. The framework is a six-stage model that entails collecting and organizing data, as well as summarizing, analyzing, and synthesizing information prior to taking a decision.

Data-driven decision-making in schools has been talked about primarily as a pursuit of administrators, who have to make top-down decisions about the allocation and distribution of resources (Breiter & Light, 2006; Massell, 1998; Schmoker, 1996). But the discussion of how to use data is changing. Advances in technology that make it possible for classroom teachers to access data open up the possibility of instructional decision making that is supported by student data. The process of using data to make fair, informed and rational educational decisions is becoming both more promising and more complex (Brunner et al., 2005). One way to conceptualize this process at all levels of the school system, including individual classrooms, is as follows:

DATA
- Stage 1: first, appropriate data has to be collected. Much of the data currently collected consists of standardized test results, but there are increasing opportunities to gather other type of data. With the help of digital technology, schools can consider collecting performance assessments, self-assessments, diagnostic data, as well as personal information, and integrating them with standardized data to provide a fuller portrait of students. School communities have to decide which kind of data to collect, based on their assumptions about what factors might make a difference in student success.

- Stage 2: Then the data have to be organized. Standardized data are not problematic since many systems have already considered how to organize standard student assessment data. However, the newer types of data (diagnostic, performance based, etc) require an organizational scheme that will allow the data to be analyzed and reported in ways that are ultimately relevant to the teachers. Schools have to figure out how to systematize the collection of such non-standardized data by developing coding schemes and criteria for quantifying such data where possible. Classroom-based assessments have traditionally been the province of classroom teachers, but it will need to be addressed by the designers of decision-support tools.

INFORMATION
- Stage 3: When data have been organized they can be analyzed and the result is information. In addition to disaggregating by the customary variables such as gender, ethnicity, SES and program attendance, standardized data have to be disaggregated by locally relevant factors. Educators have to be able to relate it to national and local standards for the domain, be able to map strands to the curriculum covered, look more deeply at the data, such as examining the distracter patterns of individual items to understand how the test results reflect skills, content and conceptual knowledge in their students.

- Stage 4: The information obtained through analysis has to be summarized to become useful for decision-making. This process is quite different for administrators and teachers. Administrators look across data for patterns than enable them to identify needs and successes for whole classes or whole schools. Classroom teachers need deep, specific information about the relationship between lessons taught and results on the tests for individual students to use the information for instructional decision-making. For classroom teachers, this involves a new set of skills: using numbers to think about students, visualizing patterns, looking for meaningful differences and checking their own inferences and assumptions against systematic results.

KNOWLEDGE
- Stage 5: Once analyzed and summarized, the information becomes actionable, that is, it becomes knowledge. To become part of a shared data culture in schools, the knowledge has to be synthesized. Synthesis requires that the decision maker have a logic model or theory of action for which the data can become evidence. For teaching, this requires the data be integrated into a theory of learning. The teacher's ability to see connections between students' test scores on different item-skills analysis, for example, and her classroom instruction is at the heart of data-supported instruction. In particular, inputs, such as time and materials, and their relationship to outputs, such as assign-

ments and activities, has to be examined in the light of the knowledge obtained through data analysis.

- Stage 6: The synthesized knowledge gained from data analysis finally has to be used to prioritize among all available information relevant to decisions that have to be made. Since prioritizing most depend on the possible outcomes, prioritizing requires a theory of learning that can connect the evidence to possible outcomes, immediate and long-term. The data can be then used to define realistic and appropriate benchmarks and learning trajectories for students as short-term outcomes. In the U.S., for example, improvement in standardized test scores is currently the long-term outcome which defines success in our schools.

The Role of Technology
This process of data-driven decision-making can be supported by a range of technologies. We studied data warehouses, web-based interactive data reports and handheld diagnostic assessment tools. We have identified three major dimensions that have to be considered in evaluating the contribution of any technology to data-driven decision-making in schools. The dimensions are:

System Level: TEACHER ↔ ADMINISTRATOR
Educators have distinctly different data and information needs at each level of the system. Educators have different data needs shaped by the type of decisions they make (i.e. instructional, resource allocation, administrative).
- Classroom teachers need diagnostic data that goes ***deep***, identifies sub-skills or subtle changes, monitors student progress and is readily available for decision-making in daily practice.
- District or building administrators need data that goes ***wide***, allowing them to see patterns among students and teachers and to make decisions about the deployment of resources.

Leadership Focus: CONSERVATIVE ↔ REFORMER
Educators in different locations are dealing with very different kinds of issues and have to use data to make very different kinds of decisions. The guiding vision of the leadership is an important component of that decision-making process. Is the leadership attempting to change underlying model of teaching and learning? Or, is the model of teaching remaining constant and the leadership seeks to improve practice within that model?
- If building or district leadership is conservative, in that it places value and emphasis on maintaining the status quo (either because it is excellent or because they see no better solution) and expects teachers to produce student

achievement outcomes within current standards and norms, however they do it, data will be used primarily for accountability.
- If leadership is reform-minded in that it places value and emphasis on change and innovation (either from a remedial or from a progressive perspective), data will be used primarily for evaluation and feed-back on programs and approaches.

Technology Fit: UNSUPPORTIVE ↔ SUPPORTIVE
Educators are provided with an array of technologies, some of which are directly relevant and useful to their data needs when it comes to decision-making, and others maybe important to the entire system's performance, but they have little impact on actual instructional decisions. We have determined five dimensions according to which technologies intended to support data-driven decision-making in school can be described:
1. decision relevance: irrelevant ↔ crucial
2. timely feedback: delayed ↔ instant
3. access and ease: inaccessible ↔ ubiquitous
4. information opacity: opaque ↔ transparent
5. manipulation flexibility: rigid ↔ flexible

Any technology can be given a rating on those five dimensions which defines its degree of supportiveness in data-driven decision making in schools.

Use Cases: how different educators use data
Our experience suggests that there are three dimensions which could be used to categories the educational data user (Figure 1). The three dimensions – role in the school system, leadership focus and technology fit – yield eight distinct types of users. Educational leaders and the designers and producers of educational technology might keep the entire range of users in mind when they plan to design or deploy a technology to support data-driven decision making in their schools. The following figure shows the eight different user personas formed by the intersection of these three dimensions.

- *Educator A* is an administrator in a school system with reform-minded leadership, but with technology that does not really support data-driven decision making for any or all of the following reasons: The data are not relevant to the kind of decisions educators actually have to make, reports arrive too late to be useful for practical decision making, are inaccessible for technical or bureaucratic reasons, incomprehensible to educators who have not had a great deal of training in data analysis when they do arrive, and the data on which the reports are based cannot be queried or manipulated by users to answer their genuine questions.

This administrator needs a way to assess in an ongoing manner whether the initiatives instituted by the administration are having the desired effect, data, in other words, that can be easily queried and used to make complex decisions and trade-offs of limited resources.

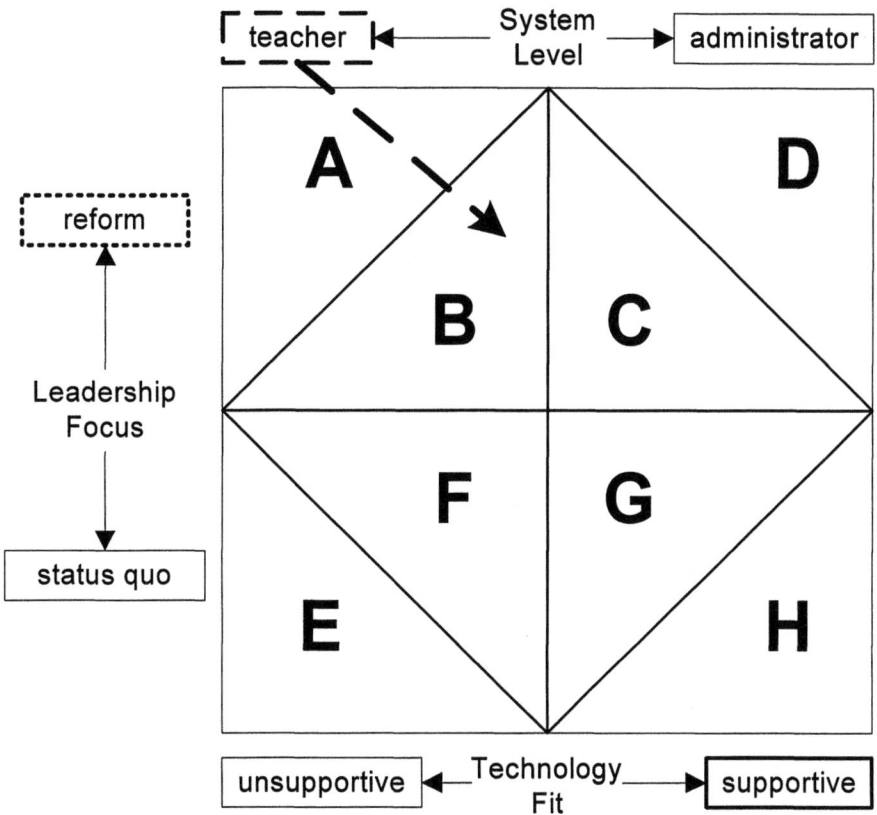

Figure 1: Categorization of Educational Use Cases

- *Educator B* is a teacher in the same kind of school, with reform-minded leadership, but poor technology for data-driven decision-making. This teacher does not need to think across students and classes and teachers, as does the administrator, but rather to think deeply about individual students and their learning needs. It is less important to her/him how a students does on a standardized test compared with a local or national norm – or even with the rest of the class – than it is to determine where the student is stuck or where mastery has occurred and the students can be pushed to try more challenging material. None of the standardized test results from the previous academic year that arrive at some point in the fall are really useful for this kind of instructional decision-making. The reports provide an overview of sorts, but it is hard to figure out how to make good use of them because it is too late to use the data to develop instructional plans either for groups or individuals.

This teacher needs a genuinely easy way to keep track of and make shareable a set of diagnostic measures and informal indicators that are perhaps related to the summative data in the standardized tests, but are the product of real on-the-ground instructional decisions: how much time, energy and resources to put into which instructional practices and to be able monitor student progress to ensure that the instructional plan is having the intended effect.

- *Educator C* is also a teacher in a school with reform-minded leadership, but with genuinely supportive technology. In this school, they are using visualization tools that allow this teacher to keep track of all kinds of ad-hoc data as well as systematic diagnostic data, and to use it to plan for differentiated instruction and to make sure that students are being supported in practicing less developed skills and successfully challenged to develop more advanced skills.

To use these data tools, this teacher will need a good deal of ongoing professional development because she is not really used to thinking about the students so systematically (really keeping track of informal information), or to using data to answer genuine questions to challenge her own assumptions about what is working in the classroom and for which students.

- *Educator D* is an administrator in a reform-minded school with supportive technology. There are data tools now available to support this administrator in gathering, summarizing and questioning not only summative but also formative data (ongoing diagnostic information) so that it becomes readily available and useful in the decision-making process.

This administrator needs support in learning to use those tools, a way to provide professional development to classroom teachers to collect diagnostic data systematically, and a way to guide and facilitate conversations with staff that investigate real questions and hypotheses with data rather than use it to confirm their existing beliefs and assumptions. In other words, this administrator needs an approach to using data to inform programmatic decisions, to deploy limited resources in such a way as to make a real difference in the specific challenge under discussion, which could be anything from the retention of new teachers to increases in standardized literacy test scores.

- *Educator E* is an administrator in a school where there is little pressure or incentive to change things, either because they are going well enough (in a successful, relatively affluent suburban district, for instance) or because things are muddling along, serving only a portion of the population, but there is no incentive to try anything new or different. The available technology to deal with data for decision-making is focused on providing evidence for the necessary mandated annual progress rating required by the government. There is no direct relationship between the achievement data collected in standardized tests, local data such as attendance and grades, and the kinds of decisions that have to do with programming and resource allocation.

This administrator needs a vision of how data tools can help use available resources more effectively, a way to experiment with collecting meaningful diagnostic data and learning to investigate possible connections between achievement data and instructional decisions. In affluent multi-ethnic communities, the real issue is likely to be how to serve ALL children, not just the ones who thrive in the current system and create the satisfactory school report card compared with national norms. In a poorer school district in which things are limping along but not critical (i.e., no threat of immediate takeover by the state), the issue is likely to be how to think more innovatively about motivating both teachers and students to try new ways to teach and learn. Both issues require a set of ongoing conversations with teachers about new approaches – and a way to evaluate their success so they can be improved.

- *Educator F* is a teacher in the same kind of status quo school system described above. Data is largely irrelevant to classroom practice, except that everything hinges on and leads up to the annual standardized achievement tests. The more critical those are, the more likely the teacher is to spend a lot of time on test preparation. This teacher might welcome technology that supports drill-and-practice learning and basic skill building. He might find the achievement data produced by such software useful as a kind of diagnostic test.

This teacher needs to become part of an ongoing process of professional development with as much emphasis on new pedagogical approaches and the integration of new media into the curriculum as on data analysis and interpretation, to make data-driven planning for more differentiated learning and teaching a genuine possibility.

- *Educator G* is a teacher in a school with similar leadership emphasis on maintaining the status quo. In this case, however, technology is available to support data collection, interpretation and analysis so that the results are a meaningful check on which students are learning and which ones are falling through the cracks.

  This teacher may know which students are learning and which ones are struggling with any given part of the curriculum, but he may not know what to do about it. This teacher needs professional development to widen his teaching repertoire so that the students who are currently failing to meet standards can be supported in new ways. Data-driven decision-making can then become a result of having both the assessments that indicate who needs help and the pedagogical approaches and materials to provide it in a more differentiated manner.

- *Educator H* is an administrator in a school in which there is little emphasis on change and innovation but there is plenty of good, supportive technology available to help make rational, data-driven decisions to ensure the maintenance of the satisfactory status quo. In places where the schools are considered good, where the majority of the students perform at or above national averages, innovation is often looked at with a good deal of skepticism. Data-driven decision-making sounds like a good idea in that context, but is hardly essential, since the way decisions have been made before highly disaggregated data became available have apparently done the job well enough. As long as the achievement data do not indicate a downward shift, it is up to individual administrators to decide on interesting, new programs and initiatives and to use informal evaluations as a way to justify and publicize such programs.

Even in affluent school districts, disaggregating data, using technologies to look for patterns in data to explain pockets of failure (classrooms or schools or populations that are not doing well according to standardized data) is increasingly part of an administrators' job, when decisions have to be made about how to distribute limited resources, whether dollars or master teachers. Such data investigations can provide a basis for justifying decisions to school board members, staff, and the community at large, even if they still have little direct impact on classroom practice and the daily decisions made about what students will do and how they will learn.

Technology Support
The dimensions along which the technology can be evaluated make sense for only half of the eight use cases described above, namely teachers and administrators in schools with a sufficiently robust technical infrastructure. There are many schools equipped with that infrastructure, schools that have data warehouses, use web-based reporting and, in some cases, handheld tools for gathering and analyzing diagnostic data, but these schools do not necessarily know how to use it for optimally data-driven decision-making,.

Much of the standardized test score data in powerful data warehouses lacks essential *relevance* to the kinds of decisions that have to be made on both the administrative and the classroom instructor level. The data serve to provide accountability information required for reporting to supervising agencies on the state and national level. Over time, the data can serve to establish "merit" scores for individual teachers and for schools as a whole: the higher the aggregated test scores, the "better" the teacher and the school. These school "report cards" can have a powerful impact on children and communities, and the results of the tests may dictate general areas of focus (e.g., literacy or mathematics), but they do not tell any teacher or administrator what to do to affect the next year's results.

The major factor working against the use of warehoused data for decision-making is the complexity of the interface. Teachers need a great deal of professional development to be able to read and interpret the available data. Data interfaces are rarely flexible enough to allow anyone but a data expert in the school system to create new reports (answering other questions). Even in a district where such requests for new and different data analyses are welcome, it takes a long time to get feedback. Educators who are trying to learn how to think *with* data need the power to "mess around" with the data they understand to see how it can be questioned in different ways. Much of the professional development related to data warehouses is primarily technical in nature, teaching educators how to gain access to the data, but not what to do with it.

The web-based interactive reports that allow teachers, parents and administrators to "drill down" into data sets and examine individual student performance on different topic strands, are often difficult to access. One issue is logistical: access to the actual server and knowing how to navigate the interface. Much of the kind of thinking teachers and administrators do, that could use a basis in data, happens when they are not in reach of a desktop computer with Internet access. Handheld devices, whether Pads or cell phones, promise to make access more ubiquitous, as it becomes increasingly possible to view and manipulate Internet-based information anywhere. More pressing, however, is the issue of logical rather than logistical access. Educators may successfully navigate to the site where the data are housed, but have no way to question the data because they do not understand what it really means. The data are opaque, in other words, rather than transparent. You have to know a great deal about what questions it can and, equally important, can NOT answer, in order to use it appropriately.

Even well designed data warehouses and interactive reports that serve administrators are not yet flexible enough to address the needs of classroom teachers. Being able to "drill down" to see an individual student's score on a single test months earlier is obviously not very useful for daily instructional practice. It may point to a plan for differentiated instruction, but it does not help track progress. Diagnostic information, both formal (classroom test scores) and informal (coded performance assessments and observations), has to become part of the picture, which means that classroom teachers have to be able to upload such data easily into the warehouses.

Finally, even a complete set of valid and reliable data about students does little to help teachers make data-driven decisions unless they have the tools that allow them to question those data in meaningful ways. Most classroom teachers are not used to or trained in ways to think with and about data. They are, at best, in a position to use the reports generated by the district to reinforce their own assumptions about why some students fail and some succeed in learning. New visualization tools that allow them to add their own data and then literally "play" with the data by asking questions and getting immediate feedback about how a set of attributes (from informal observations to literacy scores) are distributed across their students, enables teachers to challenge their assumptions with data during the decision-making process. To make this data-query process useful, however, teachers need ongoing professional development that helps and challenges them to use data to make decisions about instructional practices and to check on their assumptions (and informal observations) to evaluate the success of the interventions they have tried.

As a first step in the process of supporting professional development for data-driven decision-making in classrooms as well as schools, we are currently designing an interactive tool, which allows educators to perform a self-assessment about the extent to which the technology available in their schools is supporting the data-driven decision-making. This assessment is likely to be quite different for teachers and administrators, even though the kinds of technology supports we studied all offer information for both levels of the school system. Generally speaking, the technological supports currently in schools are far better at enabling administrators to make decisions based on data patterns across classes and schools than they are at helping classroom teachers make instructional decisions based on data for individual students. It is our hope that this tool will be useful for educators trying to make a rational decision about the use of technology and the necessary professional development to support genuinely data-driven decision-making at all levels of the school system.

References:

Ackoff, R.L. (1989). From Data to Wisdom. Journal of Applied Systems Analysis, 16, 3-9.

Breiter, A., & Light, D. (2006). Data for School Improvement: Factors for designing effective information systems to support decision-making in schools. Educational Technology and Society, 9(3), 206-217.

Brunner, C., Fasca, C., Heinze, J., Honey, M., Light, D., Mandinach, E. & Wexler, D. (2005). Linking Data and Learning. The Grow Network Study. Journal of Education for Students Placed At Risk, 10(3), 241-268.

Massell, D. (1998). State Strategies for Building Capacity in Education: Progress and Continuing Challenges (CPRE Research Report No. RR-41). Philadelphia: Consortium for Policy Research in Education.

Schmoker, M.J. (1996). Results: The key to continuous school improvement. Alexandria, VA: Association for Supervision and Curriculum Development.

Projekt VERA: Ergebnisorientierte Unterrichtsentwicklung durch internetgestützte externe Evaluation?

Ingmar Hosenfeld, Ursula Koch, Jana Groß Ophoff & Frank Scherthan

Abstract
Das Projekt VERA (http://www.projekt-vera.de) führt in sieben Bundesländern am Ende der dritten bzw. kurz nach Beginn der vierten Klassenstufe flächendeckend in allen Grundschulklassen Vergleichsarbeiten in den Fächern Mathematik und Deutsch durch. Von flächendeckenden Schulleistungsstudien verspricht man sich insbesondere Anregungen der Schulen zu ergebnisorientierter Schul- und Unterrichtsentwicklung. Außerdem kann das Projekt VERA dazu beitragen, die informationstechnischen Kompetenzen der Lehrkräfte zu verbessern, da die Nutzung des Internet für die Durchführung der Vergleichsarbeiten notwendig ist: So laden die an VERA teilnehmenden Lehrkräfte über das Internet Testaufgaben und Korrekturanweisungen herunter und geben anschließend die Resultate der Kinder online ein. Die aufbereiteten Ergebnisse und weitere, die Auseinandersetzung unterstützende Informationsmaterialien werden über das Internet distribuiert. Ergänzend können die Lehrkräfte an Online-Befragungen teilnehmen. Das Nutzerverhalten kann überdies anhand von Serverstatistiken und Logfile-Analysen analysiert und bewertet werden.

Der vorliegende Beitrag soll Einblicke in die internetgestützte Realisierung des Projektes VERA geben, allgemeine Erfahrungen und einzelne Befunde darstellen und mögliche Verbesserungs- und Unterstützungsmaßnahmen zur Diskussion stellen.

Das Projekt VERA
Das Projekt „Vergleichsarbeiten in der Grundschule in Mathematik und Deutsch (VERA)" ist eine zentrale Erhebung, in der in den beteiligten Bundesländern flächendeckend die Lernstände in den beiden Fächern jährlich abgebildet werden (http://www.projekt-vera.de). Organisiert und wissenschaftlich verantwortet wird das Projekt von einem Team an der Universität Koblenz-Landau, Campus Landau, finanziert wird es von den Bundesländern[1]. Bis einschließlich 2006 erfolgte die Erhebung jeweils zu Beginn des 4. Schuljahres, ab 2008 werden die Vergleichsarbeiten zum Ende der 3. Klassenstufe durchgeführt. In der Über-

---

1 Bis 2006/2007 Berlin, Brandenburg, Bremen, Mecklenburg-Vorpommern, Nordrhein-Westfalen, Rheinland-Pfalz und Schleswig Holstein, ab 2007/2008 alle Bundesländer.

gangsphase im Jahr 2007 erfolgt die Durchführung schon überwiegend Ende des 3. Schuljahres, in Brandenburg noch Anfang der Klassenstufe vier[2].

In Abgrenzung zu stichprobenbasierten Studien wie z.B. IGLU oder PISA, die in erster Linie dem System Monitoring dienen, wird für flächendeckende Lernstandserhebungen wie VERA ein unmittelbarer, handlungsleitender Nutzen für die Schul- und Unterrichtsentwicklung (Rolff, 2001) erwartet. In diesem Sinne ist es ein zentrales Ziel des Projektes, dass die teilnehmenden Lehrkräfte Ziele, Inhalte und Methoden des Unterrichts auf Grundlage der empirisch ermittelten Leistungsstände und entsprechender Vergleichswerte reflektieren und ggf. ihre curricularen Schwerpunktsetzungen anpassen. Daneben erlauben die Vergleichsarbeiten eine Verortung der Klassen mit Blick auf die in den Bildungsstandards definierten Anforderungen und stellen eine Grundlage für weitergehende Lernbedarfsdiagnosen dar (für weitere Ziele und Funktionen von Vergleichsarbeiten siehe EMSE, 2006).

Die Administration eines Projektes dieser Größenordnung (Beteiligte im Jahr 2006: ca. 2.300 Schulen mit 5.000 Klassen, 106.000 Schüler/-innen und 6.400 Lehrkräften) erfordert zur Distribution der notwendigen Materialien und zur Abwicklung der anfallenden Kommunikation den Rückgriff auf das Internet. Dies kann aus Sicht der Lehrkräfte eine Erschwernis darstellen, welche u.a. vermittelt über die Akzeptanz die intendierte Nutzung der Vergleichsarbeiten einschränken oder unterbinden kann.

Dabei lässt sich der Zyklus des Projekts grob in drei Phasen unterteilen:
1. Vorbereitung der Vergleichsarbeiten
2. Durchführung der Vergleichsarbeiten
3. Rezeption und Nutzung der Vergleichsarbeiten

In der ersten Phase werden in interdisziplinär zusammengesetzten und von Mitarbeiter/-innen des Projektes geleiteten Arbeitsgruppen Aufgaben entwickelt, empirisch geprüft und zentral zu einheitlichen Aufgabenheften für die Vergleichsarbeiten zusammengestellt. Im Fokus dieses Beitrages stehen jedoch die zweite und dritte Phase des VERA-Zyklus. Für diese Phasen wird im Folgenden ausführlich dargestellt, welche Schritte von den beteiligten Lehrkräften erwartet werden, wie die hinter dem VERA-System liegende Technik aufgebaut ist und welche Befunde über die Bewältigung der Technik und die intendierte Nutzung der zurückgemeldeten Ergebnisse von VERA vorliegen.

---

2 In den Jahren 2006 und 2007 wurden die Vergleichsarbeiten aufgrund der bevorstehenden Umstellung des Erhebungszeitpunktes nicht in allen sieben Ländern flächendeckend durchgeführt.

Zur Rolle des Internet aus Sicht der VERA-Lehrkräfte

Damit der VERA-Zyklus von den Schulen vollständig und möglichst störungsfrei durchlaufen werden kann, brauchen die an VERA teilnehmenden Lehrkräfte lediglich Zugriff auf einen internetfähigen Rechner samt Drucker, auf dem zum Anzeigen und Ausdrucken der Materialien der Adobe Acrobat Reader (möglichst in Version 5.05 oder neuer) benötigt wird. Außerdem haben die Lehrkräfte folgende Aufgaben mit Hilfe der VERA-Internetplattform zu bewältigen:

Zu Beginn der zweiten Phase (Durchführung der Vergleichsarbeiten) melden sich die Lehrkräfte im passwortgeschützten Bereich des Internetportals www.projekt-vera.de an und können im „Probelauf" das System kennen lernen. Dabei geht es primär darum, sich mit dem Aufbau der Internetseiten und den technischen Voraussetzungen vertraut zu machen. Im nächsten Schritt werden grundlegende Stammdaten der Klassen erhoben, d.h. die Lehrkräfte geben noch vor dem Termin der Vergleichsarbeiten Schul-, Klassen- und Schülerdaten sowie Informationen zum sozialen Hintergrund ein. Anschließend werden die Aufgabenhefte sowie die zugehörigen Korrekturanweisungen zum Download angeboten[3]. Zusätzlich besteht die Möglichkeit, eine Vorhersage abzugeben, in welchem Umfang die einzelnen Aufgaben von den Kindern der eigenen Klasse gelöst werden. Nach den Vergleichsarbeiten erfolgt zunächst die schulinterne Auswertung der Testhefte und Online-Eingabe der Schülerresultate.

Etwa zwei Wochen nach Abschluss dieser Dateneingabe beginnt schließlich die oben beschriebene dritte Phase des VERA-Zyklusses: Die ersten aufbereiteten Ergebnisse (Basisrückmeldung: z.B. Verteilung der Fähigkeitsniveaus auf Klassenebene, siehe Abbildung 1) können im Internetportal abgerufen werden. Die Ergebnisse auf Länderebene und der sog. faire Vergleich (erweiterte Rückmeldung, vgl. Helmke & Hosenfeld, 2005) werden nach der Befragung und Auswertung einer sog. Zentralstichprobe (Zufallsstichprobe beteiligter Schulen, deren Kontext intensiver untersucht wird) etwa 10-12 Wochen nach der Vergleichsarbeit zur Verfügung gestellt. Ausgehend von diesen beiden Rückmeldungswellen sollen sich die Lehrkräfte mit den Ergebnissen auseinander setzen, daraus Annahmen über Ursachen bilden und diese überprüfen sowie ggf. Maßnahmen zur Schul- und Unterrichtsentwicklung einleiten (Hosenfeld, 2005; Hosenfeld, Groß Ophoff & Bittins, 2006). Den Abschluss eines VERA-Durchgangs markiert etwa sechs Monate nach der Vergleichsarbeit eine freiwillige, internetgestützte Evaluationsbefragung, in der die Lehrkräfte Auskunft über die Rezeption und Nutzung der VERA-Ergebnisse geben (Groß Ophoff, Koch, Hosenfeld & Helmke, 2006; Koch, Groß Ophoff, Hosenfeld & Helmke, 2006).

---

3 in einigen Bundesländern entfällt dieser Schritt, da die Materialien zentral gedruckt und postalisch verteilt werden

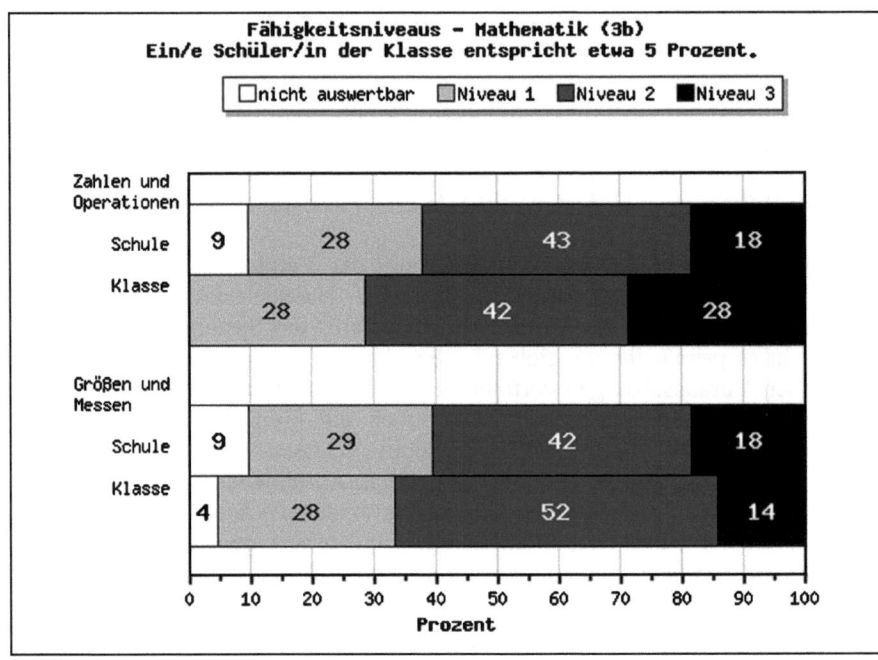

Abbildung 1: Beispiel einer Ergebnisrückmeldung (Fähigkeitsniveaus auf Klassenebene)

Technische Infrastruktur des VERA-Projektes
Für die internetgestützte Durchführung von VERA stehen an der Universität Landau insgesamt drei Server mit 100 Mbit Internet-Anbindung zur Verfügung. Zwei dieser Rechner stellen dabei das eigentliche VERA-System dar, indem ein Rechner als Webserver und der zweite als reiner Datenbankserver fungiert. Der dritte Rechner übernimmt zur Erhöhung der Ausfallsicherheit die Aufgaben der beiden anderen Server, d.h. dass auf diesem gleichzeitig sowohl Web- als auch Datenbankdienst zur Verfügung stehen und so bei Ausfall eines Primärrechners eine schnelle Umschaltung des Systems ermöglichen. Jeder einzelne Rechner ist mit zwei 2,8 GHz Xeon Prozessoren und 2 GB Arbeitsspeicher ausgestattet und hält die Daten auf drei Festplatten mit je 160 GB Kapazität vor. Die Festplatten werden hierbei als Raid5 betrieben, d.h. die Daten werden auf den drei Platten so verteilt gespeichert, dass beim Ausfall einer der Platten das System weiterhin funktioniert. Als Betriebssystem wird auf allen Rechnern SUSE Linux eingesetzt. Als Webserver dient Apache2, als Datenbankserver MySQL. Die einzelnen ausgelieferten Webseiten werden dynamisch mit PHP generiert (klassisches LAMP-System: **Linux, Apache, MySQL, PHP**).

Projekt VERA: Internetgestützte externe Evaluation 53

Das VERA-Internetportal wurde seit Beginn der Projektlaufzeit kontinuierlich weiterentwickelt und nach Usability-Gesichtspunkten optimiert. So ermöglicht z.B. ein dem VERA-Zyklus angepasstes Menü am oberen Bildschirmrand das gezielte Anspringen der einzelnen Seiten. Zusätzlich wird in einer Statusbox angezeigt, welche Aufgaben zu erledigen sind.

Während des gesamten Ablaufs der Vergleichsarbeiten (Phase 2 & 3) steht den Lehrkräften ein per E-Mail erreichbarer Support-Service zur Verfügung, der außerdem in den zeitkritischen Phasen bis zur erweiterten Rückmeldung telefonisch erreichbar ist. Zur Verwaltung und Bearbeitung der eingehenden Anfragen wird dabei das System OTRS (**O**pen source **T**icket **R**equest **S**ystem, siehe http://otrs.org/) genutzt, welches unter der GNU General Public License (GPL) vertrieben wird. Dieses System gewährleistet einen einheitlichen, hierarchischen sowie durch das Internetinterface ortsungebunden Zugriff auf die als Tickets abgespeicherten Anfragen. Die prioritäten- und zeitgesteuerte Verwaltung der Anfragen ermöglicht eine schnelle und passgenaue Unterstützung der Lehrkräfte, da u.a. auch bei Bedarf alle Anfragen einer Schule eingesehen werden können. Das OTRS-System ermöglicht zusätzlich eine Dokumentation des gesamten Support-Aufkommens, was z.B. zur Analyse der eingehenden Anfragen und damit in der Folge auch zur Optimierung des Angebots genutzt wird.

Ergebnisse
Zur Soft- und Hardware-Ausstattung
Die folgenden Ergebnisse zur Ausstattung der an VERA teilnehmenden Schulen stammen aus Daten, die mit Hilfe von JavaScript auf der Startseite des geschützten Bereichs registriert werden. Diese Informationen werden in anonymisierter Form genutzt, um die Internetpräsenz von VERA kontinuierlich zu verbessern.

So sind z.B. die VERA-Seiten für eine Bildschirmauflösung von 800 x 600 Pixel optimiert. In der Durchführung von VERA 2006[4] zeigte sich, dass noch bei 9,8 Prozent der Rechner eine solche geringe Auflösung eingestellt ist. In nur 78 Fällen (< 0,1% der Seitenaufrufe) fanden wir eine niedrigere Auflösung, die zu schlecht sicht- und bedienbaren Navigationselementen führt. Am häufigsten wurde eine Auflösung von 1024 x 768 Bildpunkten (67,3%) registriert.

In Bezug auf die Software sollte der verwendete Rechner mit einem Browser ausgestattet sein, der aktuelle Webtechniken unterstützt und zulässt (CSS, Cookies, Javascript). Diesbezüglich wurden 88 Programme unterschiedlicher Version registriert, von denen nur rund 4 Prozent für die Anzeige der VERA-Seiten problematisch sind (z.B. Netscape 4.75). Mit anderen Worten: Über 96

---

4 Erfassungszeitraum: August 2006 bis Januar 2007

Prozent der Seitenaufrufe erfolgten mit einem ausreichend aktuellen Browser, am häufigsten mit dem Internet Explorer 6.0 (71,6%).

Demnach sind die meisten Lehrkräfte in informationstechnischer Sicht ausreichend ausgestattet. Dass die internetgestützte Durchführung von VERA natürlich nicht völlig störungsfrei verläuft, belegen die OTRS-Statistiken: rund 33 Prozent der teilnehmenden Schulen traten 2006 mit dem VERA-Support in Verbindung. Über die Jahre hinweg sind die Supportanfragen jedoch rückläufig: In VERA 2005 kontaktierten noch 38,6 Prozent der Schulen den Support. Dass praktisch alle Schulen den Zyklus der Vergleichsarbeiten 2006 vollständig durchlaufen haben (Stand Januar 2007), spricht für die Zweckmäßigkeit und Funktionalität des Online-Angebots sowie für eine effektive Unterstützung durch den Support.

Zur Rezeption und Nutzung von VERA 2006
Die Evaluationsbefragung zu VERA 2006 wurde von Februar bis Juni 2007 internetgestützt durchgeführt, wobei die Teilnahme freiwillig war. Die Entwicklung des Fragebogens orientierte sich im Wesentlichen an dem Modell von Helmke (2004; siehe auch Groß Ophoff et al., 2006), in dem der Prozess ergebnisorientierter Unterrichtsentwicklung als eine Abfolge von der Rezeption und Reflexion der Ergebnisrückmeldungen bis hin zu daraus abgeleiteten Aktionen sowie deren Evaluation dargestellt wird.

In der Befragung wurden die Lehrkräfte mit Blick auf Rezeption und Reflexion u.a. um eine Einschätzung gebeten, mit welcher Intensität sie sich mit den Ergebnissen auseinander gesetzt und als wie verständlich und nützlich sie diese erlebt haben (vierstufige Skala von 1= „gar nicht" bis 4 = „sehr"). In Bezug auf die Aktion wurde erfragt, welche Maßnahmen zur Schul- und Unterrichtsentwicklung aus den VERA-Ergebnissen abgeleitet wurden. Zusätzlich zu den genannten Variablen wurde eine Vielzahl weiterer Informationen erfasst (u.a. Akzeptanz von Lernstandserhebungen, Nutzung von Unterstützungsangeboten), auf die hier aus Platzgründen nicht eingegangen werden kann.

Der Evaluations-Fragebogen zu VERA 2006 wurde 1.376-mal aufgerufen und von rund 23 Prozent der Schulen nahezu vollständig (max. fünf fehlende Angaben) ausgefüllt. Auf Grund der Freiwilligkeit der Teilnahme muss bei den Befragungsteilnehmern von einem überdurchschnittlichen Engagement ausgegangen werden. Dies wird durch das Ergebnis bestätigt, dass die in diesem Beitrag beschriebene Stichprobe eine höhere Akzeptanz von Lernstandserhebungen aufweist als die zufällig gezogene Zentralstichprobe (Evaluationsstichprobe: $M = 2,4$; $SD = 0,64$; Zentralstichprobe: $M = 2,73$; $SD = 0,56$; $t = 3,4$; $p \leq .002$).

Projekt VERA: Internetgestützte externe Evaluation 55

Da für die Durchführung der Vergleichsarbeiten (Phase 2) sowie die innerschulische Auseinandersetzung (Phase 3) das Internetportal von VERA eine zentrale Rolle einnimmt, werden im Folgenden die Evaluationsergebnisse unter Berücksichtigung der registrierten Seitenaufrufe berichtet. So ist in Tabelle 1 in der Spalte „Webstatistik" der prozentuale Anteil der an VERA teilnehmenden Schulen wiedergegeben, die bestimmte Ergebnisrückmeldungen im geschützten Bereich aufgerufen haben (N = 2.314 Schulen, Stand Januar 2007). In den folgenden Tabellenspalten sind Ergebnisse aus der Evaluationsbefragung zur „Intensität der Auseinandersetzung", „Verständlichkeit" und „Nützlichkeit" der Rückmeldungen wiedergegeben (aggregierte Werte). Die letzte Spalte gibt schließlich Auskunft über die niedrigste Anzahl der Angaben zur entsprechenden Ergebnisrückmeldung.

Rückmeldungs-Zeitpunkt		Webstatistik*	Evaluation						
			Intensität		Verständlichkeit		Nützlichkeit		
		f	M	SD	M	SD	M	SD	N_{min}
2 Wochen nach Dateneingabe	Fähigkeitsniveaus Schüler/-innen	92,7%	2.9	.65	3.2	.58	3.1	.74	895
	Fähigkeitsniveaus Klasse/Schule	89,4%	2.9	.70	3.2	.61	2.9	.79	892
Dezember 2006	Fähigkeitsniveaus im Landesvergleich	62,9%	2.8	.76	3.1	.68	2.7	.85	885
	Fairer Vergleich**	50,5%	2.2	.86	3.0	.79	2.5	.91	384

* Im geschützten VERA-Bereich wurden N = 2314 Schulen registriert (Stand Januar 2007).
** Der „Faire Vergleich" wurde in VERA 2007 nur in den Ländern Bremen, Mecklenburg-Vorpommern und Rheinland-Pfalz ermittelt und zurückgemeldet (n = 1268 Schulen).

Tabelle 1: Vergleich zwischen Nutzungsstatistiken (geschützter Bereich) und Angaben im Evaluationsfragebogen.

Es fällt auf, dass die Rückmeldungen auf Individual- und Klassenebene am häufigsten, nämlich von etwa 90 Prozent der Schulen, aufgerufen wurden. Nach Angabe der Lehrkräfte fand mit diesen relativ zeitnah zurückgemeldeten Ergebnissen eine intensive Auseinandersetzung (je M = 2.9) statt. Außerdem wurden sie als eher nützlich ($M_{indiv.}$ = 3.1; M_{Klasse} = 2.9) eingestuft. Obwohl die Fähigkeitsniveaus im Landesvergleich erst drei Monate nach den Vergleichsarbeiten zur Verfügung standen, wurden sie dennoch von über 60 Prozent der Schulen aufgerufen. Dabei fallen die Angaben zur Intensität ähnlich hoch wie bei den Fähigkeitsniveaus auf Individual- und Klassenebene aus. Die Nützlichkeit wurde demgegenüber vergleichsweise niedriger eingeschätzt (M = 2.7). Die Fähigkeitsniveaus im „fairen Vergleich" wurden nur von der Hälfte der Schulen aufgerufen. Außerdem ist auffällig, dass damit im Vergleich nur eine eher flüchtige Auseinandersetzung stattgefunden hat (M = 2.2) und diese Ergebnisrückmeldungen am niedrigsten in Bezug auf die Nützlichkeit eingestuft wurden (M = 2.5).

Die Häufigkeiten der Seitenaufrufe und die Angaben der Lehrkräfte in der Evaluationsbefragung verdeutlichen, dass sich die Auseinandersetzung mit den VERA-Ergebnissen insbesondere auf die Fähigkeitsniveaus der Schülerinnen und Schüler sowie der eigenen Klasse konzentriert. Dass ein besonderes Augenmerk auf dem eigenen Unterricht liegt, drückt sich auch darin aus, dass die fächerspezifisch formulierten fachdidaktischen Materialien (Projektgruppe VERA-Deutsch, 2006; Projektgruppe VERA-Mathematik, 2006) im geschützten Bereich häufiger als der Vergleich zum Land oder der faire Vergleich aufgerufen und herunter geladen wurden (Deutsch: 76.9 %; Mathematik: 92.3 % der teilnehmenden Schulen). In diesen Handreichungen werden die eingesetzten Testmaterialien, deren Bezug zu den Bildungsstandards und Fähigkeitsniveaus sowie deren Nutzung für den Unterricht erläutert, mit dem Ziel ergebnisorientierte Unterrichtsentwicklung zu unterstützen.

In diesem Sinne gaben rund 93 Prozent der Lehrkräfte in der Evaluationsbefragung an, bestimmte Maßnahmen seit VERA verstärkt zu haben. Der Fokus lag ähnlich wie im Nachgang zu VERA 2004 und 2005 auf der Wiederholung bzw. Vertiefung von Stoffgebieten, in denen schwache Ergebnisse bei VERA erzielt wurden. Außerdem gaben die Lehrkräfte häufig an, verstärkt in Folge von VERA Lern- und Arbeitsstrategien zu vermitteln, Fehler zur unterrichtlichen Weiterarbeit aufzugreifen und an individuelle Fähigkeiten angepasste Aufgabenstellungen einzusetzen. Auch die Test-Inhalte bzw. die Beschreibungen der Fähigkeitsniveaus scheinen ihren Weg in den Unterricht gefunden zu haben – so gaben viele Lehrkräfte an, häufiger an VERA-Fähigkeitsniveaus angelehnte Unterrichtsaufgaben entwickelt zu haben bzw. VERA-ähnliche Aufgaben in Klassenarbeiten einzusetzen.

Fazit
Betrachtet man die vorgestellten Ergebnisse, so kann zusammengefasst werden, dass es große Unterschiede in der technischen Ausstattung der Schulen gibt und dass technische Neuerungen die Schulen z.T. nur langsam erreichen. Alles in Allem ist über mehrere Jahre hinweg eine Steigerung der informationstechnischen Kompetenzen zu verzeichnen: Es gelingt praktisch allen Lehrkräften, die zweite Phase im VERA-Zyklus vollständig zu durchlaufen – bei gleichzeitiger Abnahme der Supportanfragen. Da die benutzerfreundliche Gestaltung webbasierter Rückmeldesysteme eine wesentliche Voraussetzung für eine pädagogi-

sche Nutzung von Lernstandserhebungen (z.B. Breiter & Stauke, in Druck) darstellt, wird das VERA-Portal weiterhin optimiert werden – und zwar insbesondere unter Berücksichtigung der Gegebenheiten auf Schul- und Lehrerseite. Flankierend dazu sollten die teilnehmenden Schulen auch während der dritten Phase der Vergleichsarbeiten begleitet werden, insbesondere damit die zurückgemeldeten Ergebnisse effektiv für den eigenen Unterricht genutzt werden können.

Zusätzlich zu den Webstatistiken belegen die Ergebnisse aus der Evaluationsbefragung, dass VERA zur Schul- und Unterrichtsentwicklung beitragen kann. Die Auseinandersetzung konzentriert sich v.a. auf die Fähigkeitsniveauverteilungen auf Schüler- und Klassenebene und zieht veränderte Unterrichtsinhalte und -gestaltung nach sich. Dass zunehmend auch an VERA angelehnte Aufgaben im Unterricht oder in Leistungskontrollen eingesetzt werden, kann jedoch mit Blick auf die in den USA geführte Diskussion zur Verengung des Curriculums in Folge von Schulleistungstests (z.B. Popham, 2001) nicht uneingeschränkt positiv gewertet werden. Nach Jerald (2006) birgt die gezielte Behandlung von Testaufgaben im Unterricht die Gefahr in sich, dass die Vermittlung umfassender Kompetenzen im Sinne von Weinert (vgl. Klieme, Avenarius, Blum, Döbrich, Gruber, Prenzel, Reiss, Riquarts, Rost, Tenorth & Vollmer, 2003) vernachlässigt wird. Damit verantwortungsvolles Unterrichten und standardisiertes Testen in einem konstruktiven Verhältnis zueinander stehen, sollte sich Unterricht auf den Kern der erzielten Kompetenzen konzentrieren (sog. "curriculum-teaching", vgl. Popham, 2001). Da es jedoch den Lehrkräften häufig schwer fällt, die Verbindung zwischen wissenschaftlichem Wissen und schulischem Handlungswissen herzustellen (Rolff, 2002), ist eine gezielte und kontinuierliche Betreuung der Schulen in sowohl fachlicher/fachdidaktischer als auch organisatorischer Sicht unerlässlich. Diese Forderung wird dadurch unterstützt, dass wir anhand von Strukturgleichungs-Modellen (Koch, Groß Ophoff & Helmke, September, 2006) zeigen konnten, dass die Wahrnehmung externer Unterstützungsangebote die Reflexion der Ergebnisrückmeldungen unterstützt, zu mehr innerschulischer Kooperation anregt und mit einer höheren Akzeptanz von Lernstandserhebungen einhergeht. Die Akzeptanz besitzt ihrerseits einen deutlich positiven Einfluss auf die Auseinandersetzung und damit auch auf das Ausmaß, mit dem Aktionen zur Weiterentwicklung des Unterrichts ergriffen werden.

Darüber hinaus wirkt sich die Kooperation im Kollegium positiv auf die schulinterne Verarbeitung der Rückmeldungen aus. Hier verspricht eine stärkere Einbindung der Schulleitungen in die Phase der Rezeption und Nutzung der Vergleichsarbeiten den Auseinandersetzungsprozess weiter zu intensivieren. Abschließend ist festzuhalten, dass einerseits die bisher verfügbaren Daten die Annahme stützen, dass VERA Prozesse der Unterrichtsentwicklung befördern kann. Anderseits wird jedoch auch deutlich, dass der Weg vom flächendeckenden Testeinsatz zur flächendeckenden Unterrichtsentwicklung noch lang ist und ein zentrales Desiderat die Aufklärung förderlicher wie hinderlicher Faktoren darstellt.

Literatur:

Breiter, A. & Stauke, E. (in Druck). Anforderungen an elektronische Rückmeldesysteme aus Nutzersicht. Empirische Pädagogik, 4.

EMSE. (2006). Positionspapier "Zentrale standardisierte Lernstandserhebungen" (Tagung des Netzwerks "Empiriegestützte Schulentwicklung" (EMSE)). Berlin.

Groß Ophoff, J., Koch, U., Hosenfeld, I. & Helmke, A. (2006). Ergebnisrückmeldungen und ihre Rezeption im Projekt VERA. In Kuper, H. & Schneewind, J. (Hrsg.), Rückmeldung und Rezeption von Forschungsergebnissen (S. 19-40). Münster: Waxmann.

Helmke, A. (2004). Von der Evaluation zur Innovation: Pädagogische Nutzbarmachung von Vergleichsarbeiten in der Grundschule. Seminar, 2, 90-112.

Helmke, A. & Hosenfeld, I. (2005). Standardbasierte Unterrichtsevaluation. In Brägger, G., Bucher, B. & Landwehr, N. (Hrsg.), Schlüsselfragen zur externen Schulevaluation (S. 127-151). Bern: h.e.p.-Verlag.

Hosenfeld, I. (2005). Rezeption - Reflexion - Aktion: Wie lassen sich Lernstandserhebungen und Vergleichsarbeiten pädagogisch nutzen? In Becker, G., Bremerich-Vos, A., Demmer, M. Maag Merki, K., Priebe, B. Schwippert, K., Städel, L. & Tillmann, K.J. (Hrsg.). Standards: Unterrichten zwischen Kompetenzen, zentralen Prüfungen und Vergleichsarbeiten (Friedrich Jahresheft XXIII 2005, S. 112-114). Seelze: Erhard Friedrich GmbH.

Hosenfeld, I., Groß Ophoff, J. & Bittins, P. (2006). Vergleichsarbeiten und Schulentwicklung (Vol. Schulmanagement Handbuch). München: Oldenburg Schulbuchverlag.

Jerald, C.D. (2006). 'Teach to the Test'? Just Say No. The Center for comprehensive School Reform and Improvement. Information. Abgerufen am 25. Juni 2007 von http://eric.ed.gov/ERICDocs/data/ericdocs2sql/content_storage_01/0000019b/80/1b/f3/ee.pdf.

Klieme, E., Avenarius, H., Blum, W., Döbrich, P., Gruber, H., Prenzel, M., Reiss, K., Riquarts, K., Rost, J., Tenorth, H.-E. & Vollmer, H. J. (2003). Zur Entwicklung nationaler Bildungsstandards. Bonn: Bundesministerium für Bildung und Forschung.

Koch, U., Groß Ophoff, J. & Helmke, A. (2006). Bedingungen der Rezeption von Ergebnisrückmeldungen – am Beispiel der Evaluation von VERA 2005. Beitrag präsentiert bei 68. Tagung der Arbeitsgruppe der Empirischen Bildungsforschung (AEPF) Sektion Empirische Bildungsforschung (DGfE), Universität München.

Koch, U., Groß Ophoff, J., Hosenfeld, I. & Helmke, A. (2006). Qualitätssicherung: Von der Evaluation zur Schul- und Unterrichtsentwicklung – Ergebnisse der Lehrerbefragungen zur Auseinandersetzung mit den VERA-Rückmeldungen. In Eder, F., Gastager, A. & Hofmann, F. (Hrsg.), Qualität durch Standards? Tagungsband zur 68. Tagung der Arbeitsgruppe der Empirischen Bildungsforschung (AEPF). Münster: Waxmann.

Popham, W. J. (2001). Teaching to the Test? Educational Leadership, 58 (6), 16-20.
Projektgruppe VERA-Deutsch. (2006). Didaktische Erläuterungen "Sprache und Sprachgebrauch untersuchen" und "Leseverständnis". Abgerufen am 03. Juli 2007 von http://vera-server.uni-landau.de/vera/download/VERA_didaktische_Erlaeuterungen_2006.pdf
Projektgruppe VERA-Mathematik. (2006). Didaktische Erläuterungen. Abgerufen am 03. Juli 2007 von http://vera-server.uni-landau.de/vera/download/VERA_M_alle_Aufgaben_didakt_Erlaeut_2006.pdf
Rolff, H.-G. (2001). Was bringt die vergleichende Messung von Schulleistungen für die pädagogische Arbeit in Schulen? In Weinert, F.E. (Hrsg.), Leistungsmessungen in Schulen (S. 337-352). Weinheim: Beltz.
Rolff, H.-G. (2002). Rückmeldung und Nutzung der Ergebnisse von großflächigen Leistungsuntersuchungen: Grenzen und Chancen. In Rolff, H.-G., Holtappels, H.G., Klemm, K. Pfeiffer, H. & Schulz-Zander, R. (Hrsg.), Jahrbuch der Schulentwicklung (Vol. 12). Weinheim: Juventa.

IT-Unterstützung der Testaufgabenentwicklung am IQB

Martin Mechtel

Einleitung

Die Länder der Bundesrepublik Deutschland sind in den letzten Jahren verstärkt bemüht, Lernstandserhebungen zu qualifizieren. Sie sollen zunehmend Indikatoren für einen umfassenden Monitoring im Bildungssektor liefern. Nachdem Bildungsstandards in den Jahren 2003/2004 definiert wurden, sollen diese nun anhand großer Aufgabensammlungen evaluiert werden.

Das IQB wurde 2004 gegründet, um vor allem diese Evaluierung zu leisten. Als eine länderfinanzierte wissenschaftliche Einrichtung übernimmt das IQB aber auch beratende Funktion in vielen Prozessen auf diesem Gebiet. Die Entwicklung von Testaufgaben steht dabei zunächst im Vordergrund. Hierzu werden bundesweit Arbeitsgruppen für die verschiedenen Schulfächer gegründet, Bewertergremien ernannt, die Aufgaben ersten Tests unterzogen um schließlich Kompetenzskalen zu entwickeln und die Testitems den Ländern zur Verfügung zu stellen. Dies ist aufgrund der Mengen der Aufgaben nur mit massiver Unterstützung der IT zu leisten.

Der Beitrag beginnt mit einer Darstellung der Prozesse der Aufgabenentwicklung, erläutert dann die IT-Lösungen dazu und diskutiert abschließend wichtige Entscheidungen auf diesem Gebiet.

Charakterisierung der Testaufgabenentwicklung

Für den Entwurf der Testaufgaben werden bundesweit Arbeitsgruppen gebildet. Die Mitglieder sind Lehrer und Lehrerinnen sowie Mitarbeiter und Mitarbeiterinnen von Länderinstituten mit schulnahen Tätigkeiten. Je nach Umfang des Projektes werden bis zu vier Arbeitsgruppen gebildet, die entweder regional orientiert sind (Nord, Süd usw.) oder nach Schultyp (Hauptschule, Realschule usw.). Zusammenkünfte der Gruppen sind stets mit recht hohen Kosten verbunden, so dass diese recht selten stattfinden und in der Zwischenzeit die Zusammenarbeit anders organisiert werden muss.

Wenn die Diskussion innerhalb einer Gruppe abgeschlossen ist, wird eine Aufgabe einer sog. Bewertergruppe übergeben. Hier erfolgt unter fachdidaktischer und psychometrischer Sicht eine Beurteilung und ggf. Überarbeitung. Anschließend werden die Testaufgaben zu Testheften zusammengestellt und in Pilotierungen eingesetzt. Pilotierung steht hier allgemein für eine Erhebung, die zwar den Charakter einer Lernstandserhebung hat, die Auswertung konzentriert sich aber auf die Eigenschaften der Aufgabe, nicht die der Personen. An dieser Stelle wird entschieden, ob die Aufgaben die nötigen Qualitätskriterien für Lernstandserhebungen erfüllen.

Für eine Erhebung sind neben den Testheften weitere ergänzende Informationen über die Variablen nötig. Der Begriff Variable steht hier für die kleinste Einheit einer Antwort, die dann in die Auswertung eingeht. Eine Aufgabe kann zahlreiche Variablen unterschiedlichster Form enthalten. Die Informationen dazu sind wichtig, um die Antworten der Testpersonen in eine computerlesbare Form zu übertragen. Dieser "Kodierung" oder "Rating" genannte Schritt kann teilweise automatisch durchgeführt werden (z.B. Erkennung von Schwärzungsgraden bei Ankreuzkästchen), teilweise sind Kodierer nötig um jede Antwort zu beurteilen und einen Code zu vergeben. Dieser recht teure Schritt kann durch die Bereitstellung ausführlicher Variableninformationen (Codebook) unterstützt werden.

Nach der Auswertung der Ergebnisse ist üblicherweise eine Dokumentation zu verfassen. Je nach Auftraggeber bzw. Partner werden Rückmeldungen bis zum einzelnen Schüler erwartet. Dieser Bereich ist jedoch in den nachfolgenden Darstellungen ausgeklammert, da das IQB hierzu noch keine IT-Unterstützung anbietet.

Testaufgabe und Testheft
Die aus statistischer Sicht günstigste Konstellation in einem Testheft ist die Aneinanderreihung unabhängiger Variablen. Diese können frei positioniert oder ausgetauscht werden. Allerdings ist dann die Messung bestimmter Kompetenzen nur eingeschränkt oder sehr ineffizient möglich. Daher ordnet man z.B. einem Lesetext mehrere Variablen zu und bildet so sog. Testlets. Die Vor- und Nachteile sind dabei jeweils im Projekt abzuwägen, für die IT-Planung ist nur wichtig, dass eine solche Gruppierung möglich sein muss.

Die nachfolgende Übersicht zeigt die Struktur einer Testaufgabe (Abbildung 1), so wie sie am IQB in allen IT-Modulen umgesetzt ist. Die Struktur folgt verschiedenen Anforderungen im Verlaufe eines Projektes:
- Aufgabe: Dies ist die Einheit aus der Sicht der Entwickler und Entwicklerinnen. Eine Aufgabe wird als Ganzes diskutiert, weitergeleitet und mit zahlreichen Merkmalen versehen.
- Stimulus: Der Lesetext, eine Grafik usw.
- Teilaufgabe: Diese Gruppe von Items wird als Ganzes in ein stabiles Layout übertragen (Vektorgrafik) und so in Testhefte eingebunden.
- Item: Auf dieser Ebene erfolgt die Beurteilung der Leistung der Testperson, und es werden zahlreiche Merkmale zugeordnet.

- Variablen: Repräsentation des Items in der jeweiligen Studie. Oft wird pro Item nur eine Variable angelegt, manchmal leitet sich die Beurteilung der Leistung der Testperson aber aus mehreren Teilaspekten ab. Die Entscheidung, ob ein Item in mehreren Variablen ausgedrückt oder für jede Variable ein gesondertes Item angelegt werden soll, ist im Einzelfall zu entscheiden.

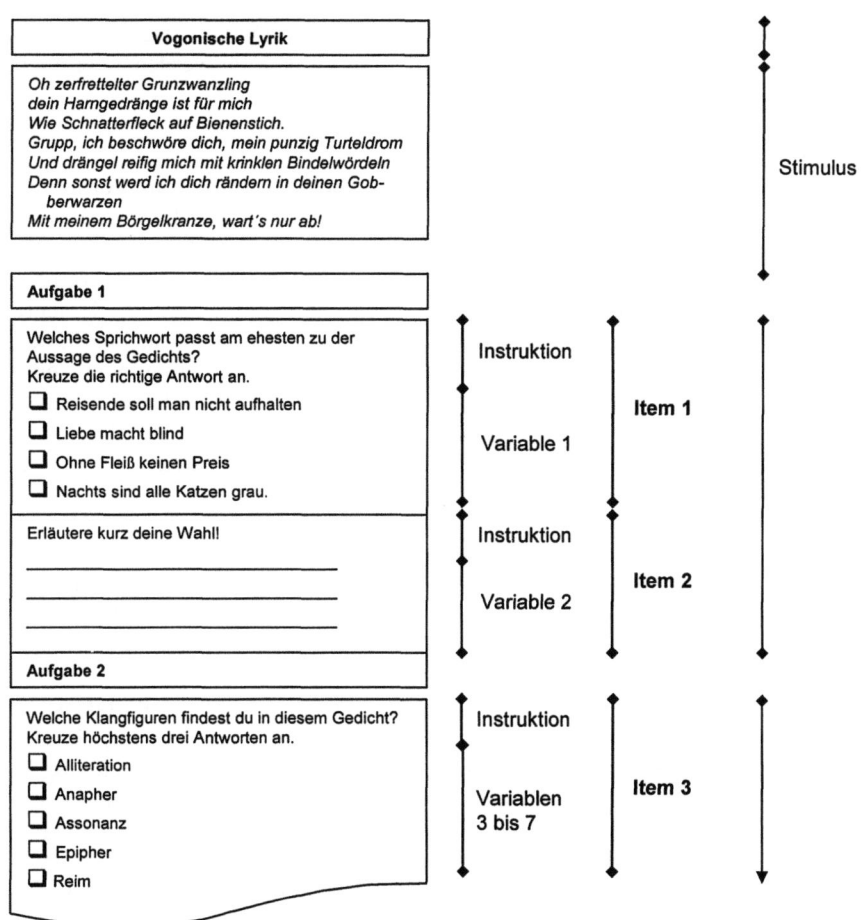

Abbildung 1: Struktur einer Testaufgabe[1]

---

[1] Der Aufgabentext enthält ein Zitat aus dem Buch „Per Anhalter durch die Galaxis" von Douglas Adams

Ein Testheft ist die Zusammenfügung von Deckblatt, einleitenden Instruktionen, Testaufgaben und anderen ggf. gewünschten Elementen. In der Testpraxis hat sich das sog. Multimatrix-Design durchgesetzt. Dahinter verbirgt sich die Festlegung, nicht allen Schülern dasselbe Testheft vorzulegen, sondern zahlreiche Testheft-Varianten zu erzeugen. Nicht alle Aufgaben sind in allen Testheften, und dann auch ggf. an unterschiedlichen Positionen. Für eine praktikable Systematik werden Aufgaben zunächst Blöcken zugewiesen. Diese Blöcke rotieren dann nach einem sinnvollen Schema in den Testheften. Durch dieses Vorgehen ist gewährleistet, dass Positionseffekte von Aufgaben erkannt werden, aber auch eine hohe Zahl von Aufgaben getestet werden kann.

Word-Formulare und Portale
Die Entwickler und Entwicklerinnen entwerfen die Aufgaben in Form von Microsoft®-Word-Dokumenten und nutzen zur Diskussion ein Internet-Portalsystem. Für die Dokumente werden speziell für die Projekte vorbereitete Formulare konstruiert. Diese Formulare erlauben die Erfassung wichtiger Merkmale (Lenkung der Aufgabenentwicklung), aber auch das Einfügen freier Elemente und Formatierungen. Die hohe Akzeptanz der Formulare ist darin begründet, dass die Nutzer eine ihnen vertraute Software benutzen. Überlegungen, eine eigene Software bereitzustellen oder gar ein Internet-basiertes Entwicklungssystem einzuführen, haben wir begraben. Der Hauptgrund dafür ist tatsächlich, dass diese Systeme Schulungsaufwand bedeuten würden und Barrieren aufbauen an Stellen, wo eine freie Entfaltung der Ideen gefragt ist.

Zu jeder Formularversion wird der Projektleitung eine Excel-Datei bereitgestellt. Diese Datei enthält VBA-Programmierung und liest die Formulardaten der Aufgabendateien eines bestimmten Verzeichnisses ein. Damit kann schnell z.B. der Anteil der MC-Items ermittelt werden.

Die Aufgabendateien werden dann in Portale hochgeladen. Das Portalsystem fußt auf ZOPE, einem Open Source Content Management System. Seiten-Templates (Präsentationsschicht) werden durch Python-Scripte (Geschäftslogik) ergänzt, die den Zugriff auf die internen Objekte (Datenschicht) gewährleistet. Die Nutzer können diskutieren, neue Versionen hochladen, ihre Aufgaben freigeben (d.h. den Bewertern übergeben) usw. Der Funktionsumfang der Portale wurde bewusst klein gehalten, um eine intuitive Bedienung zu erreichen. Die Erfahrungen sind sehr gut, der Pflegeaufwand aus Sicht der IT ist gering.

Das Portalsystem betrachtet die Aufgabendateien als normale Dateien, d.h. die darin enthaltenen Eigenschaften werden nicht ausgewertet. Über WebDAV gelangen die Aufgaben dann zum IQB.

Itemdatenbank
Übertragung der Aufgabendateien
Die Daten liegen nun also in Form von Word-Formularen vor. Als erstes werden sämtliche Teilaufgaben sowie der Stimulus mit einem Seitenlayout-Programm gestaltet und in eine Vektorgrafik überführt (EMF). Dann wird die o.g. Excel-Übersicht erzeugt, nachbereitet und anschließend über eine eigens für diesen Zweck angepasste Programmierung in die Datenbank übertragen. Dieses Verfahren ist aufwändig, und im Laufe der nächsten Projekte wird es zunehmend gelingen, die Merkmale in den Formularen vorab mit den Merkmalskatalogen der Datenbank abzugleichen und also die Übertragung zu automatisieren.

Nach der Übertragung mit Hilfe der Programmierung gibt es natürlich Wege, Aufgaben mit allen ihren Eigenschaften nachträglich über Eingabemasken einzugeben und zu ändern. Auch Grafiken können nachträglich aktualisiert werden. Für einige typische Eingabefälle sind Assistenten verfügbar, z.B. wird beim Anlegen einer MC-Variablen nur nach der Anzahl der Optionen und nach der richtigen gefragt, und anschließend sind alle Variablenvalues einschließlich Missings angelegt.

Ein weiterer Weg besteht über die sog. Datenlisten. Man kann sich für eine Auswahl von Aufgaben bestimmte Informationen als Tabelle ausgeben lassen, diese ändern und dann wieder in das System einlesen. Das spart z.B. bei Umbenennungen viel Zeit bei der Dateneingabe.

Erzeugung der Studiendokumente
Für eine konkrete Studie sind die Blöcke und Testhefte zu definieren. Dazu gibt es verschiedene Wege, da die beteiligten Wissenschaftler/innen unterschiedliche Vorstellungen davon haben, welche Informationen einfließen sollen.

Ziel ist hier eine weitgehende Automatisierung. Erster Schritt ist eine Definition der Merkmale, die bei der Auswahl der Aufgaben (bzw. korrekterweise Teilaufgaben) eine Rolle spielen. Dann generiert das System eine Übersicht, über die die Anwender mit Mausklicken und –ziehen die Aufgaben zuweisen. In Planung ist auch die Generierung eines Vorschlages, d.h. Aufgaben werden entspr. der vereinbarten Merkmale gleichmäßig verteilt. Eine wichtige Funktion des DB-Systems ist hierbei noch zu prüfen, ob unverträgliche Teilaufgaben in einem Testheft auftauchen.

Nachdem die Definition abgeschlossen ist, werden zunächst die Blöcke als Word-Dokumente erzeugt. Dieser Schritt ist notwendig, da meist noch kleinere Nachbearbeitungen nötig sind. Ziel ist natürlich, keinerlei Nachbearbeitungen vorzunehmen, aber das ist im Moment noch Vision. Denn die Entscheidung, dass diese oder jene Aufgabe doch auf einer neuen Seite beginnen soll, ist oft Geschmackssache und also nicht automatisierbar.

Wenn zusätzliche Dokumente wie Deckblätter als PDF-Datei in die Datenbank übertragen wurden, können auch die Testhefte erzeugt werden. Dies geschieht generell auf PDF-Basis, d.h. die Blöcke werden erst in das PDF-Format übertragen und dann mit den Extradokumenten zusammengebunden. Beim Binden von PDF-Dokumenten sind keine Überraschungen mehr zu erwarten, im Gegensatz zum Binden von Word-Dokumenten. Hier ist eventuell noch zu beachten, dass die Erzeugung von PDF-Dokumenten mit vorher geprüften (Adobe-)Einstellungen erfolgen sollte, damit der Druck auch die erwarteten Ergebnisse liefert.

Sämtliche Informationen zu einer Studie können als XML-Datei oder auch als XLS-Datei ausgegeben werden. Hier sind Filter und vielfältige Formatierungen möglich, die die Passung zu nachfolgenden Prozessen z.B. bei Partnereinrichtungen sicherstellen. Als Informationen stehen beispielsweise auch die Orte der Variablen in den Testheften zur Verfügung, denn das DB-System kennt ja alle Voraussetzungen zur Berechnung.

Kodierung
Für kleinere Studien, die dann Pilotierungs- oder gar Prepilotierungscharakter haben lohnt es sich nicht, Dritte mit der Kodierung zu beauftragen. Da das Datenbanksystem alle nötigen Informationen zu den Variablen kennt hat das IQB eine Kodier-Software entwickelt, die es dem Kodierer bzw. der Kodiererin erlaubt, eine Anzahl Scans schnell und verlässlich zu kodieren. Diese Anwendung wird demnächst ergänzt durch ein Werkzeug, das sowohl die Definition des Coding-Designs als auch die Aufbereitung der Ergebnisse der Kodierung unterstützt.

Architektur
Das am IQB genutzte System basiert auf MySQL als weit verbreitetes und kostenloses relationales Datenbankbetriebssystem (innoDB). Ob dieser Server auf externen Maschinen mit aufwändiger Backup-Lösung läuft oder auf einem mageren PC ist hier uninteressant. Die Ansteuerung des Datenbankservers erfolgt über einen Applikationsserver. Diese Middleware-Schicht wurde kürzlich eingeführt, um die Effizienz und die Sicherheit der Zugriffe zu erhöhen. Es handelt sich um eine .NET-VB-Anwendung, die auf einem Windows-PC laufen kann, aber auch mit Hilfe von Mono (open source project, sponsored by Novell®) auf einem LINUX-System lauffähig ist. Die Client-Anwendungen sind in .NET-VB programmiert.

IT-Unterstützung der Testaufgabenentwicklung am IQB

Das EMSE-Austauschformat
Das Netzwerk "Empiriegestützte Schulentwicklung (EMSE)" vereint Mitarbeiterinnen und Mitarbeiter auf dem Gebiet der Bildungsplanung und Schulentwicklung. Sie unterstützen nachdrücklich die mit der so genannten "empirischen Wende" verbundene daten- und wirkungsorientierte Ausrichtung von Qualitätsentwicklung und Qualitätssicherung im Bildungswesen. Dieses Netzwerk ist auch an einer Standardisierung dessen interessiert, was unter "Testaufgabe" zu verstehen ist. Da die Entwicklung der IQB-Datenbank zu einer solchen Definition zumindest aus datentechnischer Sicht führte, liegt jetzt ein "EMSE-Austauschformat" vor. Dieses zunächst gut akzeptierte Format muss sich weiter entwickeln, so wie sich die Einrichtungen entschließen, ihre Aufgaben so abzuspeichern.

Technisch handelt es sich um ein XML-Dokument (Schema-Datei liegt vor) zuzüglich weiterer Dateien (z.B. Grafiken). Sobald erste Erfahrungen vorliegen wird entschieden, ob dieses Paket als Archiv-Datei ausgetauscht wird (ZIP).

Interessanter als die technischen Aspekte sind die institutionellen. Das EMSE-Netzwerk hat eine Vorschrift beschlossen, nach der Aufgaben (resp. Items, Variablen) benannt werden, damit diese nachverfolgbar werden. Sobald das Itemformat Verbreitung findet und Items eindeutig identifizierbar werden, sollte es an jeder Einrichtung eine Auskunftsmöglichkeit geben, um den aktuellen Status oder bisherige Verwendungen zu erfahren. Es wird sich zeigen, inwieweit Transparenz hier möglich ist.

Diskussion
Warum Eigenprogrammierung?
Von den ersten Ideen bis zum derzeitigen Stand, der als recht ausgereift beschrieben werden könnte, vergingen fast 2 Jahre. Es begann mit der Recherche, welche Standards auf dem Gebiet des E-Learning zur Verfügung stehen und welche Firmen hier Erfahrungen haben. Fazit war, dass die Standards (z.B. IMS Question & Test Interoperability) viel zu umfangreich sind und im Detail nicht flexibel genug. Firmen im E-Learning-Bereich schränken vor allem die möglichen Itemformate ein, was im Schulkontext nicht akzeptiert wird. Hauptgrund jedoch war, dass keiner der Anbieter die – sicher ungewöhnliche – Erzeugung der Testhefte unterstützt.

Nun hätte man auch ein Pflichtenheft schreiben können und die Programmierung einem erfahrenen Profi-Team überlassen können. Tatsächlich gab es solche Ansätze, und die Kontakte mit Entwicklungsfirmen haben wertvolle Impulse geliefert. Nur: es war nicht möglich, vorab die erforderliche Funktionspalette zu definieren. Es wäre ein hoher personeller und zeitlicher Aufwand nötig gewesen, so etwas zu leisten, und das war nicht realistisch.

Wir hatten bereits nach einem Jahr eine Anwendung (VBA/MS-Access), mit deren Hilfe Testhefte produziert wurden. Diese frühen Erfahrungen waren für alle Beteiligten nötig, um das IT-System näher zu spezifizieren. Man darf auch nicht vergessen, dass diejenigen, die die Studie durchführen bzw. die Projekte leiten, auch lernen und im Verlauf die Prozesse optimieren. Was gestern noch günstig schien, ist heute hinderlich. Sicher wird es irgendwann eine Phase gewisser Konsolidierung geben, aber unter den beschriebenen Umständen ist es effektiver und wirtschaftlicher, die Kapazität für die Programmierung am Institut zu halten.

Warum einzelne Module statt umfassende Lösung?
Das IQB hat die Verpflichtung, seine Erfahrungen auch im IT-Bereich anderen Einrichtungen auf dem Gebiet der Lernstandserhebungen zugänglich zu machen. Die 16 Bundesländer mit den jeweiligen Instituten für Qualität in der Schule o.ä. sowie die wissenschaftlichen Einrichtungen bundesweit sind sehr heterogen bezüglich ihrer Prozesse. Nur ein modulares System mit definierten Schnittstellen kann gewährleisten, dass Items untereinander ausgetauscht werden, auch wenn z.B. nie Internet benutzt wurde.

Warum so fixiert auf die IQB-Prozesse?
Von Anfang an war die Hauptmotivation der IT-Entwicklungen, die Projekte am IQB zu unterstützen. Wir haben zwar früh den Kontakt zu den anderen Einrichtungen gesucht, es ist uns allerdings nicht gelungen, diese Kolleginnen und Kollegen stabil einzubinden. Dazu waren die Prozesse zu verschieden oder die Termine zu eng. Wenn eine Anwendung gut arbeitet heißt das leider noch nicht, dass man sie weitergeben kann. Troubleshooting kann man für das eigene Haus leisten, aber Fremde einzuarbeiten und ggf. deren Risiko mit zu übernehmen, das wäre viel verlangt.

Der Kontakt ist nach wie vor gut. Zum Ende des Jahres 2007 werden zwei Einrichtungen wichtige IQB-Module übernehmen. Der daraus resultierende Dialog wird die Systeme weiter verbessern. Ein wichtiges Feld der Zusammenarbeit ist außerdem die Definition von Merkmalskatalogen (s.u.). Die Festlegung von Merkmalen kann jede Einrichtung für sich vornehmen, wodurch hier hinreichend flexible Arbeit möglich ist.

Wie flexibel sind die Aufgabenmerkmale?
Die Frage, welche Merkmale zu einer Aufgabe (resp. Teilaufgabe, Item, Variable, Code) gespeichert werden sollten und welche nicht, ist natürlich ein zentraler

Punkt der Datenbankentwicklungen. Eine besondere Problematik ergibt sich hier, weil die Beteiligten an Lernstandserhebungen sehr unterschiedliche Auffassungen über dieselben Begriffe haben. Was ist ein Item? Welche Itemformate gibt es? An welcher Stelle des Prozesses spielt das Itemformat überhaupt eine Rolle? Wie drücke ich die Schwierigkeit aus?

Das IQB hat hier eine Zwischenlösung gewählt. Es gibt eine Reihe von festen Merkmalen, die für die Datenverarbeitung wichtig sind. Diese Merkmale haben einen festen Wertebereich, auch wenn das manchmal für Beteiligte schwer hinzunehmen ist. Beispielsweise haben wir ein Standard-Itemformat mit 5 Ausprägungen festgelegt, da hier heraus der Aufwand für die Kodierung schätzbar wird.

Wenn nun die Projektleitung überzeugt ist, dass zu einem Item weitere Formatangaben zu speichern sind, dann wird ein neues variables Merkmal angelegt. Sämtliche, für die Verarbeitung unwichtigen Merkmale liegen in sog. Merkmalskatalogen. Sie können z.B. als Filter bei der Aufgabenauswahl benutzt werden, aber intern sind die Werte neutral. Die Pflege der Merkmalskataloge ist durchaus noch offen. Bisher haben wir jeden Wunsch umgesetzt. Dadurch decken sich manchmal zwei Merkmale fast, weichen nur in wenigen Punkten voneinander ab. Allerdings können hier nur die beteiligten Fachdidaktiker bzw. Psychologen Entscheidungen treffen. Was für einen EDV-Mann deckungsgleich aussieht, ist für einen Spezialisten wie Äpfel und Festplatten. Es ist natürlich dringend geboten, hier schlanke Merkmale zu definieren und das IQB wird diese Diskussionen führen. Aber die Diskussion hierzu ist teilweise sogar eine politische.

Ausblick

Das IQB bereitet gegenwärtig intensiv computerbasiertes Testen vor (E-Assessment, Technology Based Assessment). Ausgangspunkt auch hier ist wieder die Modularisierung: Die Grafiken der Teilaufgaben, die bereits vorliegen, werden mit Adobe Flash®-Programmierung versehen und also als swf-Datei gespeichert. Diese Programmierung bietet nach außen eine einheitliche Schnittstelle, so dass Serveranwendungen jede Teilaufgabe gleich behandeln können. Operationen wie "Hat der Nutzer geantwortet?", "Speichere Antwort", "Lade vorherige Antwort" etc. können mit jedem dieser Objekte gleichermaßen ausgeführt werden. Damit ist die Aufgabe wieder austauschbar über Serversysteme hinweg.

Ob nun die Testung über Internet oder in einem Testlabor/Klassenraum stattfindet, ist zunächst nicht wichtig. Es ist wohl klar, dass in beiden Fällen ein Client-Server-System zum Einsatz kommen wird. Das IQB verfügt mit der Stiftungsprofessur "Pädagogische Diagnostik" über sehr gute Voraussetzungen, derartige Lösungen fundiert zu konzipieren und zu testen. Hardwareseitig haben wir erste Erfahrungen mit Tablet-PCs und mit Handhelds.

Die besondere Herausforderung bei computerbasiertem Testen ist die Administration. Hier bereiten wir Partnerschaften vor und werden auch international in den Austausch treten.

Weitere Planungen am IQB in Stichpunkten:
- Unterstützung der Kodierung mit einem Werkzeug zur Planung von Doppelkodierungen (s.o.)
- Unterstützung der Rückmeldungen aus den Outputs der Auswertungssoftware heraus
- Adaptives Testen
- Halbautomatisierte Zuweisung von Teilaufgaben zu Blöcken und Testheften. Dies ist theoretisch zwar gut zu bewältigen, birgt aber aufgrund der Struktur unserer Aufgaben (Testlets) besondere Hürden.

Managing with ICT in Education

Ian Selwood

Abstract
The aim of this chapter is to examine the scope, progress and limits of the implementation of ICT in Educational Management (ITEM) in England. To accomplish this aim, the nature, use of, and reasons for implementing School Information Systems (SIS) are discussed. A framework for analysing ITEM progress is presented and this is then used to analyse the development of ITEM in England. The paper concludes by drawing together lessons learnt from the English experience. Which demonstrates that progress has been slow in the implementation of SIS and while administrative use at office level and senior manager level has not been problematic. Teacher usage, and use for management purposes remains a challenge.

Introduction
Much has been written in the past decades concerning the use of Information and Communications Technology (ICT) to support teaching and learning in schools. However, the literature concerning the use of ICT to support administration and management of schools is far more limited. This chapter draws on the available literature and research carried out by the author over an extended period to examine the scope, progress and limits of the implementation of ICT in Educational Management (ITEM). To clarify the areas of concern addressed in this paper this chapter initially examines some definitions associated with Educational Management and the use of ICT to support Educational Management. The paper then continues by briefly analysing how computerised School Information Systems (SIS) can support the information and decision support needs of educational managers and teachers. A framework is then presented that enables the progress of ITEM to be analysed, and this framework is used to describe the progress that has been made in ITEM in England. The paper concludes by drawing together lessons learnt from the English experience.

Background
It is perhaps, sensible at this stage to make the distinction between administration and management. Administration can be thought of as the tasks associated with the day to day running of an organisation that ensure that the said organisation performs smoothly and efficiently to achieve its pre-determined goals. Management, however, is concerned with analysing information, making decisions, defining strategies, tactics, and goals for the organisation and ensuring that an organisation works towards these goals in an efficient and effective manner

(Fidler & Bowles, 1989). Goals and strategies will need periodic re-appraisal to ensure that they remain appropriate. However, Hodgkinson (1991) pointed out that the difference between the terms administration and management is to some degree a case of semantic convention, and that usage differs from one side of the Atlantic to the other. Furthermore, it is undoubtedly useful, on occasions, to have a single generic term to cover both administrative and management procedures; in England this term tends to be management, and this term will be used here.

Whilst generic software can be used to support the management of schools, in England all schools make use of Management Information Systems (MIS), and the international literature tends to refer to MIS used in schools as School Information Systems (SIS). It is difficult to state precisely what a computer-assisted MIS is, partly because the technology on which it is based is changing continuously, and the type of support that MIS offer, and the applications that they consist of, vary from system to system and are also continually changing. A useful working definition which concentrates on the general use of MIS is probably appropriate for our discussion:

> "…..an integrated user-machine system for providing information to support operations, management, and decision-making functions in an organisation." (Davis & Olson, 1985, p.6)

The definition stresses the need to support "management and decision making functions in an organisation" and if the organisation concerned is a school, then this would appear to be an appropriate definition for a SIS.

At the risk of over simplification, most SIS are based on the principles of a database management system, consisting of: a database, a database management system and a number of applications programs. All the data available to the specific application programs of the database system that are used for a specific purpose can be accessed and managed in an integrated way. This is particularly important for educational managers. For example, it should enable educational managers to bring together data about pupils, parents, teachers, attendance and timetable to investigate truancy by analysing data, seeking trends and patterns, hypothesising on possible reasons and forming appropriate policies. This policy, once implemented can then be analysed in a similar manner. This analysis can support educational managers in understanding and gaining insights into particular educational problems, settings, structures and operations.

In England and Wales the most widely used SIS is SIMS (http://www.capitaes.co.uk/sims) which is used in approximately 90% of schools. "SIMS is a modular but integrated system in that once entered, core data is available to other modules" (Wild & Walker, 2001, p.24). SIMS is an extremely comprehensive system that comprises of a wide range of modules and suites of applications programmes (21 modules and 5 suites of programmes for secondary schools) covering virtually all areas of school management. In most schools SIMS is networked, but even when networked some modules can be run in a limited fashion on stand-alone machines (Assessment Manager, Timetabling, and SEN) to enable more flexible or wider access to staff.

Why do Schools Implement SIS?
The goals for the introduction of SIS into schools can be summarized by stating that it is expected that they can increase the efficiency and effectiveness of, or the parts of the educational institution into which they are introduced. However, the ultimate goal for implementing an SIS must be that the education of pupils is improved. More specifically, the goals for the introduction of a SIS can be summarized as increasing the efficiency and effectiveness of the educational institution by:
- relieving teachers, management and support staff from mundane administrative tasks.
- enabling the collection and provision of accurate and up-to-date information to aid decision making and administration.
- improving the manipulation and presentation of information for different audiences.
- meeting the requirements for reporting and accountability.
- aiding in the evaluation of students, teachers and schools.

(Selwood, Wild & Millin, 1995)

SIS Usage
Administrative usage of SIS, which generally involves the automation of tasks previously carried out manually, by office staff and senior managers has not been problematic in most cases reported. However, management uses have been slow to take off. An SIS should assist educational managers in planning, organising, controlling, reviewing, monitoring and evaluating procedures and should be able to supply managers with precise and consistent information for the identification of a problem. Furthermore it should enable: the analysis of a problem into its smaller (and controllable parts); the identification of alternative solutions to the problem; the examination and evaluation of each solution's feasibility; and the ability to predict the implications of the solution (Selwood, 2004).

Most research has tended to concentrate on usage of SIS by office staff and senior managers. However, teachers are both administrators and managers and also require access to appropriately designed SIS. For example teachers need access MIS for: pupil records, recording and monitoring attendance, marking and assessment, report writing, records of achievement, monitoring pupil progress, and planning tools. (Selwood, Smith & Wishart, 2001; Selwood, 2005; Selwood & Pilkington, 2005)

A Theoretical Framework for the Development of SIS.
To trace the development and progress of ITEM in England a theoretical framework was developed (Selwood, 2004). This framework built on earlier idea suggested by Visscher (1991) who had suggested that ITEM usage generally developed through four stages. Whilst it is difficult to disagree with his first two stages 'initiation' and 'expansion' he claimed that: the third stage 'integration' can be characterised by 'integrated modules' and 'the production of management information' (Visscher, 1995); and that the fourth stage 'stabilisation', characterised by computer assistance reaching its full potential and the focus shifting to systems maintenance and refinement. In 1997 Selwood & Drenoyianni argued that these final two levels were somewhat open to debate and that it was possible that systems, even though they may comprise of "integrated modules" they may not be flexible enough to provide information for management decisions (Mitchell & Wild, 1993). Also, other considerations, such as lack of appropriate training for senior educational managers and constant revision of systems due to technological change, may inhibit management use. With the benefit of hindsight, I suggested that in England it would appear that the third level of the evolution was administration – the use of computers to aid school administration and that the fourth level is management – ICT being used to aid decision making. What I did not make entirely clear at the time was that the stabilisation level still remained but moved to become the fifth level. However, whether this level is achievable is debatable, as Visscher (2001) stated "it presupposes the accomplishment of the full potential of computer-assisted school administration and management ..." and "... software for the full support of managerial work is still elusive" and new technologies "... promote new types of support for administrative and managerial school staff" (p. 14). I therefore suggest that, as it would appear unlikely that progress in SIS will cease, the stabilisation level should be replaced with a "refinement level" where applications and uses are refined. These levels of development can thus be combined into a new theoretical framework (Figure 1).

Figure 1: Theoretical Framework for Progress in ITEM

In 2004 (Selwood) combined this new framework with the transformation model that National Council For Educational Technology (NCET) (1995) suggested for mapping the use development of ICT for teaching and learning, resulting in a new theoretical framework for mapping the progress of SIS or ITEM. This framework is now used to describe how SIS has developed in England over time.

Theoretical Framework for the Progress of ITEM:
- Evolutionary Stage
    o Initiation
    o Expansion
- Transitional Stage
    o Administration
- Revolutionary Stage
    o Management
    o Refinement

Progress in SIS usage in England.
Evolutionary Stage
Initiation Level (1960-1983 approx)
Even though, according to Visscher (1991) the initiation level for SIS is characterised by software being developed by a few amateurs working in isolation, the earliest reported use of computers for school management in England was the use of a mainframe computer to keep pupil records (Anonymous, 1968 in Bird, 1986). Also, during the period under consideration two reports were published detailing how computers could be used for pupil records to benefit local education authorities (LEAs) (Local Authority Management Services and Computer Committee (LAMSAC), 1974) and schools (BCSCC,1976), and one report on the use of computers for timetabling (LAMSAC, 1978). Research during this period was limited but Bird (1986), and Shaw & Lancaster (1986) both reported that secondary schools were using microcomputers (pre-PC) for administrative tasks, along the lines suggested by Visscher. Furthermore, some LEAs had purchased licenses for timetabling software to run on their mainframes e.g. Birmingham purchased SPL(NZ) for £12,000 in 1973 (Selwood 2004).

Expansion Level (1984-1988)
As more schools and educational authorities became aware of the potential benefits of the computer the expansion level commences (Visscher , 1991), the numbers of software packages grow, and commercial software developers start to enter the market. Microcomputers became more powerful and PCs became the standard. Shaw & Lancaster (1986) reporting on their research, undertaken in 1983/84, reported that commercial companies were beginning to develop soft-

ware, as were some LEAs (Wild & Walker, 2001). Significantly research by Streatfield & Jones (1987) showed that primary schools were beginning to make use of computers for educational management.

Transitional Stage
Administration Level (1988-1998)
The transitional stage of the development of SIS commenced in England with the Education Reform Act (ERA) (House of Commons, 1988). Even though there was no compulsion within the ERA for schools to introduce computers for administrative purposes, the implications of the Act were such that their introduction seemed inevitable. Also, the Coopers & Lybrand (1988) report on Local Management of Schools and DES Circular 7/88 (DES, 1988a), had both identified the need for schools to have computerised MIS; and the Education Support Grants (ESG) (DES, 1988b) to assist schools in introducing appropriate information systems undoubtedly boasted uptake of SIS. However, the Government did not specify systems or capabilities of systems at this time. This was left to market forces. During this stage a number of research projects were undertaken in England including: LAMSAC (1989), NCET (1993), Selwood (1995), Selwood (1996), Selwood & Drenoyianni (1997), and Wild, Smith & Walker (2001). These research projects highlighted that during this transitional stage or administration level significant changes in the use of SIS in England and Wales occurred and this was undoubtedly due in part to central government actions, though sometimes these unintentionally slowed progress. Many issues relating to the implementation of SIS occurred and recurred throughout this stage and these were: unstructured/poor implementation procedures, lack of national standards for SIS, lack of training, aptness of training, funding issues, software limitations, the need for further research and most importantly, the lack of use of systems for management purposes.

Revolutionary Stage 1998
Management Level
It is perhaps optimistic to say that England entered the management level in 1998. However, what is apparent is that from this time schools were increasingly using the data stored in their SIS to support decision making at various levels (Selwood, 2004). 'The Stevenson Report' (Stevenson Committee, 1997) and the subsequent UK government ICT initiatives (e.g. the National Grid for Learning (NGfL) (DfEE, 1997)) undoubtedly moved things forward in all areas of ICT in education. Many NGfL sites offered support to classroom teachers by way of resources, lesson plans, schemes of work, work sheets, assignments discussion forums, and on-line activities for pupils. Furthermore, in 1999 the UK government introduced its Information Management Strategy for schools, the purpose of which was to: define and control the information collected from schools and

LEAs; clarify the roles of all concerned in managing and using information electronically; set common standards for ICT systems (hardware, software and communications); and support training (DfEE, 2000).

Refinement Level 2001
Even though the management level probably started in 1998 and continues today, the refinement level is now well under way as signified by various developments. During the last decade a number of different information systems have become available to schools that may well promote the improved functioning of schools. These are the so-called school performance feedback systems (SPFSs) (Selwood & Visscher, 2007) which provide information on various aspects of the functioning of schools, e.g. student performance, staff satisfaction, the nature of instruction, school management behaviour, and cooperation amongst teachers. (e.g. PAT, PIPS, MidYIS and Yellis in England)

Usually these systems provide information on how a class/teacher/school performs compared to a reference group (e.g. the national average, similar local schools, etc.). Some SPFSs provide the views of students and teachers or of teachers and school management on the same topic which can lead to interesting varying results. The idea behind school/teacher performance feedback is of course that the recipient, when necessary, uses the feedback and tries to improve performance.

In England the government has for some time provided schools, each autumn, with data on their performance and to enable them to better analyse this data they produced the Pupil Achievement Tracker (PAT). This was sent to all schools in October 2003 on CD-ROM and regular updates have subsequently been available from the "Standards website" (www.standards.dfes.gov.uk). The PAT was built to enable teachers, and senior managers to analyse performance data, and generate information that can be used to support teaching and learning, identify pupil needs, and set targets. It allowed schools to look back at their previous performance and compare this to the results of pupils in other similar schools across the country. According to Kirkup, Sizmur, Sturman & Lewis (2005) PAT users were generally positive about "the visual presentation of data and the ability to compare groups of pupils." (p. 2). However, they also reported that many questionnaire respondents and focus group participants found PAT difficult to use and "were confused as to how to input data", and it was incompatible with their SIS. Indeed Kirkup et al. noted that rather than use proprietary systems, school based systems and Excel spreadsheets were the most popular data management tools as they were flexible in inputting internally generated data, and allowed individual pupil tracking. It should be noted that PAT has recently been replaced by RAISEonline (Reporting and Analysis for

Improvement through School self-Evaluation) (DfES, 2006) a web-based interactive tool developed by Ofsted and the DfES to replace the Performance and Assessment (PANDA) report (an annual written report to schools) and PAT.

Other significant developments that have taken place during this stage include what amounted to a re-write of SIMS in 2003/2004, and government concern regarding teacher workloads culminating in "Raising Standards and Tackling Workload: a National Agreement" (DfES, 2003). This agreement between the government and teacher unions specified what tasks teachers should not do, and where ICT should be used to undertake particular administrative and management tasks. A paper by Selwood & Pilkington (2005) discusses how ICT can be used to release teacher time.

Conclusions

It is apparent from the above that England has a long history if the use of ICT to support administration and management in schools. However, progress has been slow in implementing full SIS usage for a variety of reasons. When schools in England first started using microcomputers for administration and management tasks they were probably not powerful enough for the role, and even the early pc's had limited memory and storage. Systems were largely introduced without, what I believe to be, adequate consultation, at school level, ignoring the best practice, of systems analysis and implementation, from commerce and industry. Senior management in schools did not receive adequate education in how the systems can be best used to construct a picture of their schools performance, and plan for the future by displaying current trends and modelling different scenario. The numbers of machines, for SIS, installed under government/LEA/school funding was for a long time inadequate to directly impinge on classroom teachers. As the government left choice of software to market forces, and until recently had no overall strategy, their changes in regulations on the reporting schools were required to perform meant software had to be continually revised, not to improve performance but to meet government reporting requirements. Without a doubt the use of SIS has reduced the amount of paper work that in former days had to be carried out by school staff manually, but increased accountability has had the opposite effect. i.e. SIS implementation has led to the recording of new data because the SIS enables the manipulation of these data which can produce valuable new information.

However, regarding the retrieval and utilization of information that can be used in solving ill-structured problems we have not progressed very far as yet. Schools need more guidance on how to use the available data to aid school improvement. Training of all staff, clerical, administrative, senior managers and teachers needs to be ongoing and teachers need greater access to SIS.

References:

BCSSC. (1976). The use of the Computer as a Management Aid in Schools. Computer Education, 23, 13-17.
Bird, P. (1986). Microcomputers in School Administration, 2nd Edition. London: Hutchinson.
Coopers and Lybrand. (1988). Local Management of Schools: A Report for the Department of Education and Science. London: DES.
Davis, G. & Olson, M. (1985). Management Information Systems. New York: McGraw-Hill.
DES. (1988a). Circular No 7/88: Education Reform Act: Management of Schools. London: DES.
DES. (1988b). Education Support Grant: A Grant Circular. London: DES.
DfEE. (1997). Connecting the Learning Society. London: DfEE.
DfEE. (2000). Information Management Strategy. London: DfEE. www.teachernet.gov.uk/management/atoz/i/ims/ and www.teachernet.gov.uk/management/ims/
DfES. (2003). Raising Standards and Tackling Workload: a National Agreement. http://www.tda.gov.uk/remodelling/nationalagreement.aspx
DfES. (2006). RAISEonline. https://www.raiseonline.org/
Fidler, B. & Bowles, G. (Eds.). (1989). Effective Local Management of Schools. London: Longmans in Association with British Educational Management and administration Society.
Hodgkinson, C. (1991). Educational Leadership. Albany: State University of New York Press.
House of Commons. (1988). Education Reform Act 1988: Chapter 40. London: HMSO.
Kirkup, C., Sizmur, J., Sturman, L. & Lewis, K. (2005). Research Report No 671: Schools' Use of Data in Teaching and Learning. Nottingham: DFES.
LAMSAC. (1974). Towards a Computer Based Education Management Information System. London: LAMSAC.
LAMSAC. (1978). Computer Assisted School Timetabling. London: LAMSAC.
LAMSAC. (1989). Computer-based administration systems in Schools - July 1989: A report on the current use of information technology for Schools Administration in the context of the Education Reform Act 1988. London: LAMSAC.
Mitchell, S. & Wild, P. (1993). A Task Analysis of a Computerised System to Support Administration in Schools Educational Administration and Management, 21(1), 53-61.
NCET. (1993). Management Information Systems in Schools: a survey of current practice. An NCET Internal Report.
NCET. (1995). Managing IT – A planning tool for Senior Managers. Coventry: NCET.
Selwood, I. (1995). The Development of ITEM in England and Wales. In Barta, B.-Z., Telem, M. & Gev, Y. (Eds.). Information Technology in Educational Management. London: Chapman & Hall for IFIP.
Selwood, I., Wild, P. & Millin, D. (1995). Introduction of IT in School Management: Approaches, Preparation, Human and Political Aspects. In Barta, B.-Z., Telem, M. & Gev, Y. (Eds.). Information Technology in Educational Management. London: Chapman & Hall for IFIP.
Selwood, I. (1996). Information Technology to Record and Monitor School Attendance in Education. In The Second IFIP International Working Conference - Conference Proceedings. Hong Kong: IFIP & HKBU.
Selwood, I. & Drenoyianni, H. (1997). Administration, Management and IT in Education. In Fung, A., Visscher, A., Barta, B.-Z. & Teather, D. (Eds.). Information Technology in

Educational Management for the Schools of the Future. London: Chapman & Hall for IFIP.

Selwood, I., Smith, D., & Wishart, J. (2001). Supporting UK Teachers through the National Grid for Learning. In Nolan, C.J.P., Fung, A.C.W. & Brown, M.A. (Eds.). Pathways to Institutional Improvement with Information Technology in Educational Management. London: Kluwer for IFIP.

Selwood, I. (2004). Information Technology in Educational Administration and Management in Schools in England and Wales: Scope, Progress and Limits. Unpublished Ph.D. thesis, University of Birmingham.

Selwood I. (2005). Primary School Teachers' use of ICT for Administration and Management. In Tatnull, A., Visscher, A. & Osario, J. (Eds.). Information Technology and Educational Management in the Knowledge Society. New York: Springer.

Selwood, I. & Pilkington, R.M., (2005). Teacher Workload: Using ICT to Release Time to Teach, Educational Review, 57(2), 162-174.

Selwood, I. & Visscher, A. (2007 In press). The potential of school information systems for enhancing school improvement. In Soquel, N. & Jaccard, P. (Eds.). Governance and Performance of Education Systems. New York: Springer.

Shaw, A. & Lancaster, D. (1986). A Study of the use of Microcomputers in Secondary School Administration. Sheffield: Sheffield City Polytechnic.

Stevenson Committee. (1997). Information and communications technology in UK schools: An independent enquiry (The Stevenson Report). London: Pearson.

Streatfield, D. & Jones, S. (1987). From here to technology: Use of computers in administration and management by local education authorities. Slough: NFER.

Visscher, A.J. (1991). School Administrative Computing: A Framework for Analysis. Journal of Research on Computing in Education, 24(1), 1-19.

Visscher, A.J. (1995). 'Computer assisted school administration and management: where are we and where should we go?' In Barta, B.-Z., Telem, M. & Gev, Y. (Eds.). Information Technology in Educational Management. London: Chapman & Hall for IFIP.

Visscher, A.J. (2001). Computer-assisted school information systems: the concepts, intended benefits, and stages of development. In Visscher, A.J., Wild, P. & Fung, A.C.W. (Eds.). Information Technology in Educational Management: Synthesis of Experience, Research and Future Perspectives on Computer-Assisted School Information Systems. Dordrecht, Holland: Kluwer Academic Publishers.

Wild, P., Smith, D., & Walker, J,. (2001). Has a Decade of Computerisation Made a Difference in School Management. .In Nolan, C.J.P., Fung, A.C.W. & Brown, M.A. (Eds.). Pathways to Institutional Improvement with Information Technology in Educational Management. London: Kluwer for IFIP.

Wild, P. & Walker, J. (2001). The Commercially Developed SIMS From A Humble Beginning. In Visscher, A.J., Wild, P. & Fung, A.C.W. (Eds.). Information Technology in Educational Management: Synthesis of Experience, Research and Future Perspectives on Computer-Assisted School Information Systems. London: Kluwer for IFIP.

Second Part: Large Scale SMIS

Rückmeldesystem zur Kompetenzmessung in Ungarn

Emese Stauke

Einleitung
Die Qualitätssicherung der Bildungssysteme steht aufgrund ihrer internationalen Evaluationen mehr als je zuvor im Mittelpunkt des Interesses der empirischen Schulforschung. Die Ergebnisse der Evaluationen dienen nicht mehr nur dem Erkenntnisinteresse einzelner Forschungsgruppen, sondern haben eine wichtige Bedeutung auf jeder Ebene des Bildungssystems. Die Rückmeldung der Ergebnisse wird also immer relevanter für die Qualitätssicherung und -entwicklung.

In diesem Beitrag wird eine Form der Rückmeldung vorgestellt, die in Deutschland bis jetzt keine Anwendung gefunden hat. Die Zielgruppe der computerbasierten Rückmeldung in Ungarn sind Schulträger, Schulleitungen und Lehrkräfte. Es handelt sich dabei um eine Software, die zur Rückmeldung der zentralen Kompetenzmessung in ungarischen Schulen eingesetzt wird. Langjährige Erfahrungen auf diesem Gebiet zeichnen die ungarische Schulforschung aus. Aus diesem Grund wurde die Software im Rahmen einer größeren Untersuchung als Fallstudie ausgewählt. Folgender Beitrag gibt eine kurze Zusammenfassung dieser Fallstudie.

Rückmeldesysteme
Eine immer stärkere Output-Orientierung (Altrichter, 1998, Terhart, 2002, Kohler & Schrader, 2004) in der Bildungsforschung führt dazu, dass auf unterschiedlichen Ebenen angesiedelte Entscheidungsträger im Bildungssystem eine Fülle von gesammelten Daten zu analysieren haben, um fundierte Entscheidungen treffen zu können. „Im Kontext ausgeweiteter Dezentralisierungs- und Deregulierungstendenzen und der damit einhergehenden Stärkung schulischer Autonomie bei gleichzeitig vergrößerter schulischer Rechenschaftspflicht und Verantwortung in Europa verlassen sich Erziehungspraktiker mehr und mehr auch auf Daten, um bessere Entscheidungen hinsichtlich vielfältiger schulischer Aspekte zu treffen." (Ackeren, 2003)

Die Datensammlung hat in Deutschland mit dem sogenannten PISA-Schock begonnen, anlässlich der am 5./6.12.2001 vom KMK beschlossenen ersten Maßnahmen (KMK, 2001). Nach dem Bekanntwerden der unterdurchschnittlichen Ergebnisse im internationalen Vergleich wurden bundesweit Maßnahmen zur Kompetenz- und Leistungsmessung, zum Monitoring von Bildungsstandards und zur Selbstüberprüfung konzipiert und durchgeführt. Diese sollten nicht nur wie internationale Schulleistungsstudien die Systemebene mit Informationen beliefern, sondern auch als Input für Maßnahmen zur Schul- und Unterrichtentwicklung genutzt werden. Dadurch vergrößerte sich der Adressatenkreis der Daten. Die Ergebnisse wurden nun auch an die beteiligten Schulen und Lehrkräfte zurückgekoppelt. Diese Art von Rückmeldung und die Nutzung der Daten für eine bessere Entscheidungsfindung erfordert eine IT-Unterstützung alleine in Anbetracht der Datenmenge. Eingebettet in so genannte Informationssysteme lassen sich die Daten erfassen, analysieren und entsprechend visualisieren. Das macht eine systematische Untersuchung der Anforderungen an Informationssysteme notwendig, die schulische Leistungsdaten an die Schule oder an die Öffentlichkeit, auch „school performance feedback systems" (SPFS) (Visscher, 2002) genannt, zurückmelden. Nach Visscher können SPFS unterschiedliche Ziele für unterschiedliche Zielgruppen verfolgen, wie Rechenschaftspflicht und Schulentwicklung.

Technisch können die Rückmeldungen ungeachtet ihrer Distribution in drei Kategorien eingeteilt werden:
- Papierbasierte Rückmeldung (inklusive statische PDF-Dateien)
- Computerbasierte Rückmeldung
- Webbasierte Rückmeldung

Aus der Forschung zur Software-Ergonomie (Balzert, 1988; Crawford, 2002; Europäische-Kommission, 1990; Karat, 1996; Maaß, 1993; Peschke, 1988; Preece, Rogers, & Sharp, 2002; Redder, 2000) und den Erkenntnissen aus dem Human-Centered Design (Karat, 1996; Carroll, 2002; Crawford, 2002; Preece, Rogers, & Sharp, 2002) ist seit längerem bekannt, dass Informationssysteme immer an die Bedürfnisse der Nutzerinnen und Nutzer angepasst werden und wietere Qualitätskriterien der Softwareentwicklung entsprechen müssen (vgl. Breiter & Stauke, in Druck).

Eine systematische Untersuchung der Rückmeldesysteme und das Sammeln von Erfahrungen bei der Nutzung geben weitere Hinweise zur Gestaltung von SPFS. Die folgende Fallstudie leistet einen Beitrag zu dieser Untersuchung.

Sie ist Teil einer größeren Untersuchung, in der mehrere technische Lösungen zur Ergebnisrückmeldung betrachtet und verglichen werden. Dabei geht es um die Erhebung von Anforderungen an ein technisches Rückmeldesystem für Leistungsergebnisse, wobei sich die Analyse an folgenden Vergleichskriterien orientiert:
- Ziel des Systems (Für welchen Zweck wurde es entwickelt?)
- Zielgruppe (Wer soll vorrangig mit dem System arbeiten?)
- Distribution (Auf welchem Weg werden Daten an wen verteilt?)
- Plattform (Unter welchem Systemvoraussetzungen läuft das System?)

- Funktionsumfang (Welche Funktionen sind enthalten?)
- Datenerfassung (Wie wird die Datenerfassung realisiert?)
- Datenanalyse (Wie wird die Datenanalyse realisiert?)
- Visualisierung (Wie wird die Datenvisualisierung realisiert?)

Die ungarische Testserie, die in diesem Artikel aufgrund ihrer computerbasierten Unterstützung als Fallstudie dargestellt wird, heißt „Országos Kompetenciamérés" („Kompetenzmessung"), und wird in den sechsten, achten und zehnten Jahrgängen in Ungarn durchgeführt. Die Ist-Analyse basiert auf Desk-Research und Prozessanalyse durch Interviews mit dem ausführenden Forschungsinstitut (Értékelési Központ) und Lehrkräften aus ungarischen Schulen.

Historie der ungarischen Leistungsmessung im internationalen Vergleich
Leistungsvergleichsstudien sind in der ungarischen Schulforschung kein unbekanntes Terrain. Seit Anfang der 70er Jahre wurde die Teilnahme der ungarischen Schulen an internationalen Studien als Mitgliedstaat der IEA (International Association for the Evaluation of Educational Achievement) gefördert. Seitdem gibt es eine systematische Überprüfung der Output-Leistung des Schulsystems in unterschiedlichen Lernbereichen, wie Lesen, Mathematik, Naturwissenschaften, Computerkompetenz, etc. Das Ziel der IEA-Studien ist eine empirische Basis für die Untersuchung der nationalen Bildungssysteme der Mitgliedsstaaten zu liefern und dadurch eine Vergleichbarkeit zwischen ihnen zu ermöglichen (IEA, 2007). Abbildung 1 zeigt, an welchen internationalen Studien Ungarn teilgenommen hat.

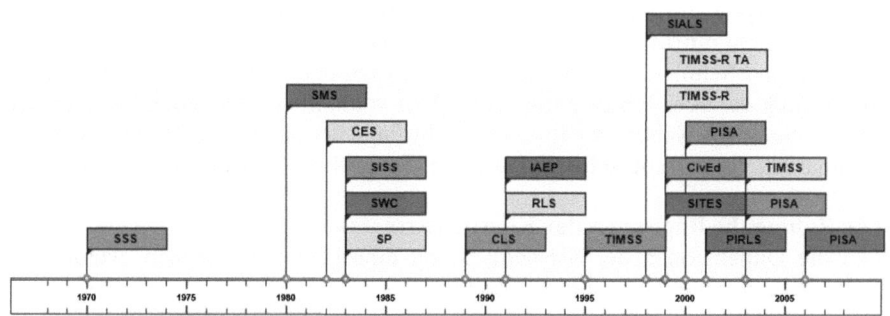

Abbildung 1: Zeitleiste der internationalen Vergleichsstudien mit ungarischer Beteiligung (In Anlehnung an Báthory, 2003)

Anhand der Daten aus den Systemuntersuchungen („system level evaluation" Báthory, 2003) kann die Bildungsforschung des jeweiligen Landes weitere Evaluationen konzipieren, die dann Erkenntnisse über den Zustand, die Verteilung

lung und den Entwicklungstrend der Lernleistung der nationalen Bildungsteilnehmerinnen und -teilnehmer liefern. Diese Art von Erhebung hat ebenfalls eine lange Tradition in Ungarn.

Die so genannten Monitor-Untersuchungen wurden erstmalig in 1986 und ab 1991 alle zwei Jahre durchgeführt und liefern Informationen für die Bildungspolitik und -forschung auf Grund von empirischen Daten über den Lernstand der jeweiligen Population. Die Schülerinnen und Schüler wurden in den Bereichen Lesen, Mathematik, Informationstechnische Grundbildung und in den Naturwissenschaften geprüft (Tabelle 1).

Jahr	Lesen	Mathematik	ITG/ Informatik	Naturwissenschaften
1986	4, 8, 10, 12	4, 8, 10, 12	8, 10, 12	--
1991	4, 8	4, 8	8	--
1993	10	10	10	10
1995	3, 4, 7, 8, 10, 12	3, 4, 7, 8, 10, 12	8, 10, 12	--
1997	4, 6, 8, 10, 12	4, 6, 8, 10, 12	4, 6, 8, 10, 12	4, 6, 8, 10, 12
1999	8	8	8	--
2001	4, 8	4, 8	8	4, 8
2003	8	8	8	8
2005	8	8	8	8

Tabelle 2 Die Monitor-Untersuchungen in den Fächern und Jahrgangsstufen

Der zweijährige Zyklus ermöglicht eine longitudinale Beobachtung der jeweiligen Schülerpopulationen. Die Schulforscher hatten also schon vor der PISA-Untersuchung ein umfassendes Bild über den Leistungsstand der ungarischen Schülerinnen und Schüler. Defizite im Bereich Lesen und Verstehen wurden bereits am Anfang der 90er Jahren aufgedeckt (Vári et al., 2000). Dennoch hat auch der ungarische PISA-Schock zu einer neuen Auflage der nationalen Untersuchungen diesmal auf der methodischen Basis von PISA geführt (Horn & Kiss, 2006).

Die Rahmenbedingungen der Kompetenzmessung
Um die Dimensionen der Messung besser einschätzen zu können, werden im Folgenden die Zahlen der Tests dargelegt.

Die getestete Population umfasste im Jahr 2006 114.207 Sechstklässler, 113.092 Achtklässler und 108.686 Zehntklässler. Beteiligt an der Erhebung waren ca. 2.000 Schulträger mit ihren 3.800 Schulen und 4.200 Standorten.

Die Tests wurden landesweit am gleichen Tag in den Fächern Mathematik und Leseverstehen ausgeführt.

Rückmeldesystem zur Kompetenzmessung in Ungarn 87

Der Datenabgleich für die Testvorbereitung (Anzahl der Klassen und Klassengrößen) lief über eine Online-Plattform, auf der jede Schule die Datenlieferung durchführen musste. Anhand dieser Daten wurden die Testhefte gedruckt und per Botenpost an die Schulen geliefert. Hier wurden die Tests jedes Jahr von den Lehrkräften der Schule nach einem vorgegebenen Protokoll ausgeführt.

Das softwarebasierte Rückmeldeverfahren
Die ausgefüllten papierbasierten Test- und Fragebögen werden anhand der Stichprobenliste sortiert und 20 im Vorfeld nach dem Zufallsprinzip ausgewählte Testhefte pro Jahrgang und pro Schule werden in die Zentrale des Forschungsinstituts nach Budapest eingesendet. Hier werden sie von den Experten ausgewertet. Die Analyse der Stichprobe ergibt dann die Vergleichswerte für die Auswertung der Daten in den Einrichtungen.

Alle Daten, die zentral ausgewertet wurden, werden gemeinsam mit den errechneten Vergleichswerten in die Datenbank des Auswertungstools aufgenommen. Die so entstandene Software wird auf CD (per Post) oder per Download im Internet an die Schulen verteilt.

Die Zielgruppen der softwarebasierten Auswertung sind die Schulträger, die Schulen und ihre Lehrkräfte. Berichte auf unterschiedlichen Aggregationsniveaus stehen zur Verfügung.

Der Schulträger-Bericht zeigt die aggregierten Ergebnisse der Schülerinnen und Schüler der jeweiligen Schulträger, die an ihren Schulstandorten achten und zehnten Jahrgänge haben.

Der Bericht besteht aus drei Teilen:
- Vergleich der eigenen Ergebnisse mit den Ergebnissen anderer Schulträger
- Vergleich der Schulen des Schulträgers untereinander
- Zustand der Standorte und die Zusammensetzung der Schülerschaft im Einzugsgebiet des Schulträgers

Der Vergleich der Ergebnisse der Schülerleistung geschieht über die standardisierten Durchschnittswerte (nach dem PISA-Muster[1]). Die Schulträger können die Ergebnisse der eigenen Schulen aufgrund der Standardpunkte einordnen. Sie können also von verschiedenen Diagrammen ablesen, wie viel Prozent der ungarischen Schulträger signifikant bessere und schlechtere Ergebnisse als die eigenen erzielt haben. Weiter wird die Verteilung der Kompetenzen als Boxplots-

---
1   Die ermittelten Testleistungen werden auf einer Leistungsdimension abgetragen, die jeweils durch einen Mittelwert von 500 und eine Standardabweichung von 100 definiert werden. Diese Definition ist beliebig. (Baumert, Stanat & Demmrich, 2001)

Diagramm dargestellt und gleichzeitig mit den Durchschnittswerten des Landes, der Region, vergleichbar großer Orte und gleicher sozialer Zusammensetzung verglichen (siehe Abbildungen 2, 3 und 4).

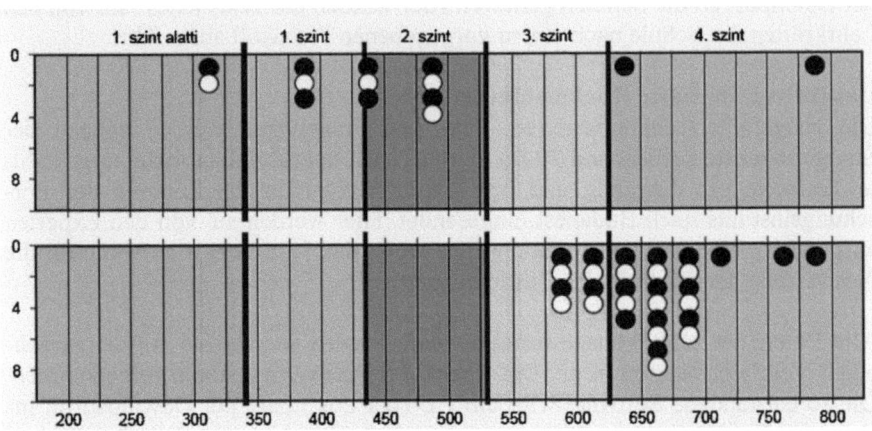

Abbildung 2: Verteilung der Kompetenzstufen (von eins bis vier) aufgrund der Standardpunkte in zwei Schülergruppen (jeder Punkt steht für eine/n Schüler/in)

Im dritten Teil des Berichtes bekommen die Schulträger Informationen über
- den Zustand der Schulstandorte im Einzugsgebiet
- die Anzahl von Fachräumen
- über den sozialen Hintergrund der Schülerschaft
- Index der Zusammensetzung der Schülerschaft
- Disziplin- und Motivationsindex der Schülerinnen und Schüler

Die Ergebnisse dieser Befragung werden in Diagrammen mit den Durchschnittswerten anderer Schulträger verglichen.

In allen weiteren Reports (Schul- und Standortreport) sind die gleichen Daten nur auf anderen Aggregationsstufen repräsentiert. Bei dem Schulbericht werden die Schule mit anderen Schulen und die Schulstandorte einer Schule unter sich verglichen, bei den Schulstandorten geschieht der Vergleich mit anderen Schulstandorten und unter den eigenen Klassen.

Neben den bereitgestellten Standardberichten können die Lehrkräfte die weiteren in die Stichprobe nicht eingeflossenen Testdaten in das System eingeben und somit die Auswertung für die individuelle Schule vervollständigen. Sie erhalten die oben beschriebenen Berichte mit den aktualisierten Daten.

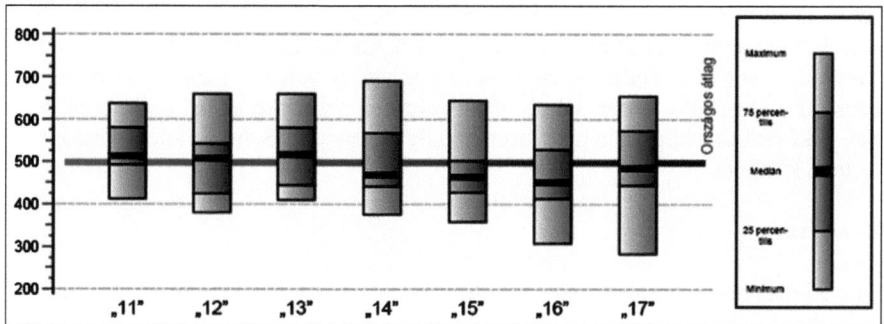

Abbildung 3: Vergleich der Kompetenzverteilung in allen Klassen eines Schulträgers mit Hilfe von Boxplots

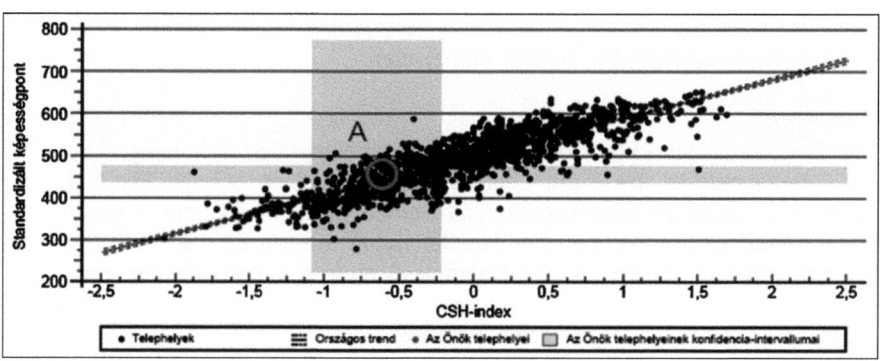

Abbildung 4: Trendanalyse mit Hilfe der Index zur sozialen Zusammensetzung der Schülerschaft

So bietet das Programm auch eine schülerindividuelle Analysemöglichkeit, die aber in der Datenhoheit der Schule bleibt.

Sind die Daten vollständig erfasst, können zur Analyse weitere Kontextdaten hinzugezogen werden. In der Standardauswertung werden folgende vordefinierte Kontextdaten verwendet:
- Schultyp
- Ortschaftstyp (Hauptstadt, Stadt, Dorf)
- Größe des Ortschaftstyps (groß, mittel, klein)

Darüber hinaus können eigene Kontextdaten definiert und erfasst werden. Solche Daten können die unterschiedlichen Unterrichtskonzepte oder das Geschlecht oder dem Migrationshintergrund[2] abbilden. Durch diese Attribute können Lerngruppen zusammengestellt werden, deren Leistung mit den gleichen Methoden wie die Zentralstichprobe ausgewertet werden kann. Das bedeutet, dass die Lehrkräfte in der Schule ihre Vergleichsgruppen selbst definieren können und dadurch die Leistung ihrer Schülerinnen und Schüler auch besser einordnen können.

Bewertung
Ziel
Das Ziel des ungarischen Rückmeldesystems ist die Rückmeldung der zentral erfassten Stichprobe und die dazugehörenden Auswertungen sowie die Möglichkeit der Erfassung der nicht in die Stichprobe gefallenen Datensätze und deren Auswertung. Das System konzentriert sich auf die Ergebnisse der landesweiten Kompetenzmessung und auf Umgebungsvariablen, die per Fragenbogen im Zuge der Messung erfasst worden sind. Es werden keine weiteren Tests oder Leistungsergebnisse in die Analyse einbezogen.

Zielgruppe
Die Zielgruppe der Entwicklung sind die teilnehmenden Schulträger, Schulen und Schulstandorte sowie die Lehrkräfte der einzelnen Schule. Die Software richtet sich nicht an Schülerinnen und Schüler mit ihren Eltern sowie an die Schulöffentlichkeit. Vorrangig sollen die Lehrkräfte an den Schulen mit dem System arbeiten, indem sie die Ergebnisse eintragen und die Auswertungen analysieren und dadurch Informationen für die eigenen Schul- und Unterrichtsentwicklungsprozesse dargeboten bekommen.

Distribution
Distribution der Softwarelösung erfolgt hauptsächlich per CD und auf dem Postweg vom Értékelési Központ an die Schule geschickt. Die Zugangsdaten bekommen die Schulen schon zu Beginn der Tests ebenfalls auf dem Postweg. Die gesamte Software oder die entwickelten Updates werden auf der Webseite des Forschungsinstituts als Download bereitgestellt. Durch die gewählte Distribution entsteht eine „gefühlte" Sicherheit bei den Lehrkräften und eine höhere reale Datensicherheit als bei Internet-Anwendungen.

Plattform
Die Software läuft unter dem Betriebsystem Windows und benötigt die Version Windows 2000 mit Service Pack 3 oder Windows XP Service Pack 2. Für den

---

2   Nach der Definition des ungarischen Minderheitengesetzes leben in Ungarn 13 anerkannte Minderheiten, davon sind zwölf nationale und eine ethnische Volksgruppe. Dies entspricht insgesamt 8-10% der Bevölkerung. Die zahlenmäßig größte Minderheit sind die Romas, ihre Migration in das Bildungssystem ist gesetzlich geregelt.

Betrieb der Software ist die Anwendung Microsoft .NET-Framework in Version 2.0 erforderlich. Eine plattformunabhängige Entwicklung ist in Ungarn wegen der homogenen Computerausstattung der Schulen nicht notwendig.

Funktionsumfang
Neben der Generierung der Berichte beinhaltet der Funktionsumfang die Datenerfassung mit einer einfachen Benutzerschnittstelle zur Eingabe der Testergebnisse. Diese können ebenfalls über eine Importschnittstelle aus dem Microsoft-Excel-Format in die Datenbank eingetragen werden und in die Datenanalyse einbezogen werden. Eine webbasierte Lösung ist nur als Unterstützungsangebot vorgesehen.

Datenerfassung
Die Eingabemaske zur Datenerfassung orientiert sich an dem Aufbau des Testheftes und ist damit ein Wiedererkennungseffekt.

Datenanalyse
Ein Nachteil des Rückmeldeverfahrens ist die zweistufige Datenanalyse. Zuerst erfolgt die Auswertung der Daten, die in die zentrale Stichprobe eingeflossen sind, durch Experten des Értékelési Központ mit statistischen Hilfsmitteln und die Bereitstellung der Datenbank. Durch diesen Schritt verzögert sich die Rückmeldung im Gegensatz zu einer webbasierten Echtzeit-Lösung um mehrere Monate. Eine zeitnahe Rückmeldung, die für die Unterrichtentwicklung erforderlich ist (Breiter & Light 2006), wird dadurch nicht möglich. Die zweite Phase der Datenanalyse basiert auf der ersten Phase als Grundlage und wird in den Schulen durchgeführt. Nach der Dateneingabe erscheint das Ergebnis sofort in den zur Verfügung gestellten Diagrammen.

Visualisierung
Die Visualisierung der Informationen erfolgt über statische einfach gestaltete, gut lesbare und ausführlich dokumentierte Diagramme. Die Beschreibungen und Beispiele zur Interpretation bieten Hilfestellung bei der Auswertung. Bei den generierten Diagrammen gibt es keine weitere Möglichkeit zur spielerischen Analyse und Veränderungen. Die Lehrkräfte können die Ergebnisse zu jeder Aufgabe analysieren und dadurch nach Fehlerursachen suchen. Dagegen ist ein Längsschnittsvergleich der Ergebnisse der Kompetenzmessung nur über zwei Jahre möglich.

Bei der vorgestellten computerbasierten Rückmeldung bleibt die Datenhoheit bei den ausführenden Schulen. Das nimmt ihnen das Gefühl der Kontrolle durch die Schulbehörde, was ein wesentlicher Grund für die Akzeptanz der Messung in der Einführungsphase war. Die Software bietet keine Möglichkeit des Schulrankings, nur des Vergleiches mit den repräsentativen Durchschnittswerten.

Durch die Vergabe der Implementierung an eine externe Firma kann sich das Forschungsinstitut Értékelési Központ auf ihr Kerngeschäft konzentrieren und gleichzeitig die Anforderungen hinreichend definieren. Insgesamt lässt sich über die Entwicklung eine positive Bilanz aus technischer und funktionaler Sicht ziehen. Über die genaue Nutzung der Software wurde nach Aussage des Instituts bis jetzt keine Untersuchung geführt.

Ausblick

Um das Bild über das Rückmeldesystem der ungarischen Kompetenzmessung vervollständigen zu können, sollte noch eine ausführliche Untersuchung zur Nutzung durchgeführt werden. Diese sollte auf die Fragen der Nutzerzufriedenheit und weiteren Verbesserungen und Änderungen eingehen. Die in der Auswertung formulierten negativen Aspekte könnten als Hypothese in die Befragung einfließen. Durch eine stichprobenbasierte repräsentative Umfrage kann die durchschnittliche Nutzung ermittelt und Viel- bzw. Wenignutzer identifiziert werden, wobei dann die Erfahrungen mit dem System und die Gründe der Nichtnutzung aufgedeckt werden können. Teilnehmende Beobachtungen bei der Nutzung des Systems können die Methodentriangulation vervollständigen.

Literatur:

Ackeren, I. v. (2003). Evaluation, Rückmeldung und Schulentwicklung: Erfahrungen mit zentralen Tests, Prüfungen und Inspektionen in England, Frankreich und den Niederlanden. Münster [u.a.]: Waxmann.
Altrichter, H. (1998). Reflexion und Evaluatioon in Schulentwicklungsprozessen. In Altrichter, H., Schley, W. & Schratz, M. (Eds.). Handbuch zur Schulentwicklung (pp. 703). Innsbruck [u.a.]: Studien-Verl.
Balzert, H. (Ed.). (1988). Einführung in die Software-Ergonomie. Berlin u.a.: Campus.
Báthory, Z. (2003). Rendszerszintü pedagógiai felmérések. Iskolakultúra, 2003(8), 3-19.
Baumert, J, Stanat, P. & Demmrich, A. (2001). PISA 2000: Untersuchungsgegenstand, theoretische Grundlagen und Durchführung der Studie. In Baumert, J., Klieme, E., Neubrand, M., Prenzel, M, Schiefele, U., Schneider, W., Stanat, P, Tillmann, K. & Weiß, M. PISA 2000. Opladen: Leske + Budrich.
Breiter, A., & Light, D. (2006). Data for School Improvement: Factors for designing effective information systems to support decision-making in schools. Educational Technology & Society, 9 (3), 206-217.
Breiter, A., & Stauke, E. (in Druck). Anforderungen an elektronische Rückmeldesysteme aus Nutzersicht. In Hosenfeld, I. & Groß Ophoff, J. (Eds.). Nutzung und Nutzen von Evaluationsstudien in Schule und Unterricht (Vol. 21(4)). Landau: Empirische Pädagogik.

Carroll, J. M. (Ed.). (2002). Human-Computer Interaction in the New Millennium. New York: ACM Press.
Crawford, C. (2002). The Art of Interactive Design: A Euphonious and Illuminating Guide to Building Successful Software. No Starch Press.
Europäische-Kommission. (1990). EU-Bildschirmrichtlinie (90/270/EWG). Luxemburg: Europäische Kommission.
Horn, D., & Kiss, N. (2006). A tanulás elösegítése és az iskolavezetés - Részlet az OECD "Improving School Leadership" Programjának magyar országtanulmányából. Új Pedagógiai Szemle, 2006(11).
IEA.Studies. (2007). Abgerufen am 31.10.2007 von http://www.iea.nl/studies.html
Karat, J. (1996). User Centered Design: Quality or Quackery? Interactions, 3(4), 18-20.
KMK. (2001). Erste Konsequenzen aus den Ergebnissen der PISA-Studie. Abgerufen am 31.10.2007 von www.kmk.org/aktuell/pm011206.htm#ref1
Kohler, B., & Schrader, F.-W. (2004). Von der externen Evaluation zur Entwicklung von Schule und Unterricht. In Kohler, B. & Schrader, F.-W. (Eds.). Ergebnisrückmeldung und Rezeption (Vol. 18, pp. 3-18). Landau: Empirische Pädagogik.
Maaß, S. (1993). Software-Ergonomie. Benutzer- und aufgabenorientierte Systemgestaltung. Informatik Spektrum, 16, 191 – 205.
Peschke, H. (1988). Partizipative Entwicklung und Einführung von Informationssystemen. In Balzert, H. (Ed.). Einführung in die Software-Ergonomie (pp. 299-322). Berlin u.a.: Campus.
Preece, J., Rogers, Y., & Sharp, H. (2002). Interaction Design: Beyond Human-Computer Interaction. New York: John Wiley & Sons.
Redder, V. (2000). Medienergonomische Gestaltung von Online-Informationssystemen. Unpublished Diss., Universität Bremen, Fachbereich Mathematik/Informatik.
Terhart, E. (2002). Wie können die Ergebnisse von vergleichenden Leistungsstudien systematisch zur Qualitätsverbesserung in Schulen genutzt werden? Zeitschrift für Pädagogik, 48, 91-110.
Vári, P., Bánfi, I., Felvégi, E., Krolopp, J., Rózsa, C., & Szalai, B. (2000). A tanulók tudásának változása I. Új Pedagógiai Szemle, 2000(6).
Visscher, A. (2002). A Framework for Studying School Performance Feedback Systems. In Visscher, A. (Ed.). School improvement through performance feedback. Lissa: Swets & Zeitlinger.

Schulstatistik oder Management Information System?

Pius Bischofberger

Eingliederung der Bildungsstatistik Kanton Zürich
In der Schweiz liegt die Bildung in der Hoheit der Kantone. Die Bildungsstatistik des Kantons Zürich ist Teil der Bildungsplanung und gehört damit zum Generalsekretariat (Stab) der Bildungsdirektion (Kultusministerium). Dies ermöglicht den Kantonen, Reformvorhaben auf die lokalen Gegebenheiten abzustimmen und schneller auszuführen. Den Nachteil der verschiedenen Schulsysteme versucht man durch gemeinsame Projekte – wie z. B. HarmoS (Harmonisierung des Schulunterrichts bezüglich Schulstufen und Bildungsstandards) – und Konkordate zu minimieren. Ein neuer Bildungsartikel der Bundesverfassung kann unter bestimmten Umständen die Kantone zur Harmonisierung zwingen (siehe www.bi.zh.ch → Organigramm der Bildungsdirektion).

Die Eingliederung der Bildungsstatistik in den Stab erlaubt dieser, die Schulstatistiken aller Stufen vom Kindergarten bis zur Hochschule zu bearbeiten. Sie hat damit auch eine koordinierende Funktion und kann Ämter übergreifende Projekte realisieren, wie z. B. die Plattform „Schul- und Berufswahl" (SBW), eine Webapplikation zur Koordination der Tätigkeiten von Lehrpersonen und Berufsberatungen mit Individualdaten der Lernenden.

Anderseits ist die Bildungsstatistik ausnahmsweise nicht im Statistischen Amt des Kantons eingegliedert, wodurch sie stark problembezogen operieren kann und eine überschaubare, kreative Größe hat (gut 6 Vollpensen).

Umfang der Bildungsstatistik Kt. ZH
Von den 1.25 Millionen Einwohnern des Kantons wird von der Schulstatistik gut ein Fünftel individualstatistisch erfasst. Unter strenger Einhaltung der gesetzlichen Grundlagen werden seit 1999 personifizierte Angaben zur Ausbildung, zu Abschlüssen und seit 2006 auch vollumfänglich zu sonderpädagogischen und unterrichtsergänzenden Maßnahmen erhoben. Jede Person erhält von der Bildungsstatistik einen Identifikator, der die Analyse von Bildungsverläufen vom Kindergarten bis zur Hochschule ermöglicht. Die Daten werden in einer relationalen Datenbank verwaltet. Wenn der vom schweizerischen Parlament beschlossene neue Personenidentifikator eingeführt ist, werden wir ihn für die Schulstatistik verwenden.

www.bista.zh.ch

Seit 2004 unterhält die Bildungsstatistik (Bista) eine Website, eingebettet unter „Zahlen und Fakten" in der Website der Bildungsdirektion (www.bi.zh.ch). Damit verfolgen wir verschiedene, insbesondere auch interne Ziele. Über das öffentlich zugängliche Glossar und Datenaufbereitungen legen wir interne Standards für Definitionen und Standardabfragen fest. Diese Abgrenzungen mögen trivial erscheinen, sind es aber keineswegs, da verschiedene Interessengruppen (Schulen, Parlament, Verwaltung und Controlling) unterschiedliche Bedürfnisse haben (Abgrenzung privat – öffentlich, Volksschule – Sonderschule, Obligatorische Schulzeit – Volksschule etc.).

Nicht nur als Dokumentationssystem, sondern auch als Informationssystem dient die Website internen und externen Zwecken. Das neu eingeführte Öffentlichkeitsprinzip gibt dem Bürger Einblick in die Informationen der Verwaltung, sofern nicht ein nachweisbares Datenschutzbedürfnis dies verbietet. Über das Web möchten wir den größten Teil der allgemeinen Informationsbedürfnisse verschiedenster Gruppen abdecken, um die personellen Ressourcen für die übrigen Aufgaben frei zu halten.

Noch bevor die Bista Website eingerichtet war, wurde im Jahr 2003 im Rahmen eines kantonalen eGov Projektes eine webbasierte Erhebungsplattform angeboten. Diese musste zwar aus diversen Gründen wieder geschlossen werden, nicht zuletzt, weil die erforderlichen Daten einfacher aus Schulverwaltungslösungen über eine Standard Schnittstelle elektronisch importiert werden können. Im Rahmen der neuen Website planen wir für 2008 eine Webapplikation einzuführen, insbesondere für die Erfassung der „Sonderpädagogischen und unterrichtsergänzenden Maßnahmen" (SOP Erhebung, 135 000 Lernende).

Über eine reine Erhebungsplattform hinaus geht die auf anfangs 2008 geplante webbasierte Kommunikationsplattform „Schul- und Berufswahl" (SBW). Sie wird die beiden letzten Schuljahre (8./9. Schuljahr) sowie die „Brückenangebote" (freiwilliges „10. Schuljahr") umfassen und soll die Kooperation zwischen Lehrpersonen und Berufsberatungen fördern und erleichtern. Schul-, klassen- und schülerbezogen wird Beratung und Findung einer Anschlusslösung unterstützt. Als Nebenprodukt liefert diese Applikation ohne Zusatzaufwand die Daten der seit 2005 durchgeführten SOS Erhebung („Schüler Ohne Schulanschluss", per Ende März, klassenbasiert über Web) und der seit 2000 existierenden, individualbasierten „Papier"-Erhebung, die den Stand der Wahl per Ende des Schuljahres erfasst.

(Wenn nicht explizit erwähnt, beziehen sich nachfolgende Referenzen immer auf www.bista.zh.ch)

Schulstatistik oder Management Information System? 97

Zwang zur Offenlegung kann zum Entscheid führen, bestimmte Daten erst gar nicht zu erheben.
- Das Primat der Politik kann einschränkend wirken. Ein MIS für die Verwaltung/Regierung, auf welches das Parlament keinen Zugriff hätte, kann es nicht geben. Ein MIS würde den Handlungsspielraum der Regierung einengen.
- Der KEF ZH (Konsolidierter Entwicklungs- und Finanzplan) stellt Ziele und Indikatoren zur Zielerreichung in der Form dar, wie sie dem Parlament von der Regierung angeboten wird. (vgl. → Überblick → Entw. & Finanzplan)

Bista versus Operatives System (ERP)
- Im Gegensatz zu einem ERP deckt die Bildungsstatistik nur wenige operative Tätigkeiten der Verwaltung ab. Beispiele dafür sind die Anzahl der bewilligten Vollzeitstellen für die Schulgemeinden (abhängig von der Anzahl Schüler und vom Sozialindex der Gemeinde, vgl. → Übersicht → Sozialindex), die Einforderung der Rückvergütung von den Gemeinden für die Schüler des Untergymnasiums oder die Bestimmung von Klassengrössen in der Berufsbildung, abhängig von der schulischen Herkunft der Lernenden (→Berufsbildung → Schulniveau Index)
- Im Gegensatz zu einem ERP ist das Informationssystem der Bista für einen kleinen Benutzerkreis geschrieben. Es ist im Vergleich zu einem ERP viel spezifischer und bietet für den Anwender weniger Komfort und Sicherheit.

Neben der Bedeutung und dem Gewicht, welches das System durch die Abdeckung operativer Anwendungen erhält, wird dadurch auch Genauigkeit erforderlich, was sich auf die Qualität des Gesamtsystems positiv auswirkt.

Systementwicklung
Ein zweites Spannungsfeld ergibt sich für die Bista bei der Systementwicklung. Diese bewegt sich zwischen Polen, wie sie für Verwaltung, Universität und private Unternehmen typisch sind.

Bista und universitäres Umfeld
- Eine Verwaltungsstelle kann kaum je in dem Masse Forschung und Innovation betreiben wie das an einer Universität möglich ist, so wünschenswert das auch wäre.
- Der Wissenstransfer von den Hochschulen zur Praxis ist nicht immer optimal.
- Der Hochschule obliegt die „Kür". Die Kontinuität in der Pflege von Know how und Tools ist aber nicht immer sichergestellt.

Zwang zur Offenlegung kann zum Entscheid führen, bestimmte Daten erst gar nicht zu erheben.
- Das Primat der Politik kann einschränkend wirken. Ein MIS für die Verwaltung/Regierung, auf welches das Parlament keinen Zugriff hätte, kann es nicht geben. Ein MIS würde den Handlungsspielraum der Regierung einengen.
- Der KEF ZH (Konsolidierter Entwicklungs- und Finanzplan) stellt Ziele und Indikatoren zur Zielerreichung in der Form dar, wie sie dem Parlament von der Regierung angeboten wird. (vgl. → Überblick → Entw. & Finanzplan)

Bista versus Operatives System (ERP)
- Im Gegensatz zu einem ERP deckt die Bildungsstatistik nur wenige operative Tätigkeiten der Verwaltung ab. Beispiele dafür sind die Anzahl der bewilligten Vollzeitstellen für die Schulgemeinden (abhängig von der Anzahl Schüler und vom Sozialindex der Gemeinde, vgl. → Übersicht → Sozialindex), die Einforderung der Rückvergütung von den Gemeinden für die Schüler des Untergymnasiums oder die Bestimmung von Klassengrössen in der Berufsbildung, abhängig von der schulischen Herkunft der Lernenden (→Berufsbildung → Schulniveau Index)
- Im Gegensatz zu einem ERP ist das Informationssystem der Bista für einen kleinen Benutzerkreis geschrieben. Es ist im Vergleich zu einem ERP viel spezifischer und bietet für den Anwender weniger Komfort und Sicherheit.

Neben der Bedeutung und dem Gewicht, welches das System durch die Abdeckung operativer Anwendungen erhält, wird dadurch auch Genauigkeit erforderlich, was sich auf die Qualität des Gesamtsystems positiv auswirkt.

Systementwicklung
Ein zweites Spannungsfeld ergibt sich für die Bista bei der Systementwicklung. Diese bewegt sich zwischen Polen, wie sie für Verwaltung, Universität und private Unternehmen typisch sind.

Bista und universitäres Umfeld
- Eine Verwaltungsstelle kann kaum je in dem Masse Forschung und Innovation betreiben wie das an einer Universität möglich ist, so wünschenswert das auch wäre.
- Der Wissenstransfer von den Hochschulen zur Praxis ist nicht immer optimal.
- Der Hochschule obliegt die „Kür". Die Kontinuität in der Pflege von Know how und Tools ist aber nicht immer sichergestellt.

Dabei bedingen sich die Ziele gegenseitig: Nur bei hoher Lieferbereitschaft, Qualität und Nutzwert werden Analysen angefordert. Häufigkeit und Vielfalt der Analysen ihrerseits bringen die notwendige Erfahrung, bringen Feedback und Einsicht in die Verwendung der Auswertungen und fördern schliesslich die Qualität.

Man kann sich natürlich fragen, ob es Ziel einer Verwaltungseinheit sein kann, die Nachfrage zu steigern. Nach unseren Erfahrungen können wir unseren Aufwand durch das Anbieten von Standard Informationen über die Website gering halten. Effektiv erheben und verarbeiten wir heute weit mehr als das Zehnfache an Information mit kürzeren Lieferzeiten und höherer Qualität zu geringeren Gesamtkosten als 1998, vor der Einführung der Individualstatistik.

Zusammenfassung und Ausblick
Die Bista Zürich versucht, aus ihren Daten möglichst vielen Interessenten möglichst grossen Nutzen zu erbringen mit der Überzeugung, dadurch die Qualität der Daten und der Analysen zu erhöhen, und mit der Hoffnung, so letztlich der Bildung zu dienen. Speziell die Verwendung der Daten für operative Aufgaben erzwingt Präzision. Verwaltungsintern werden die Daten beispielsweise für die Schulbeurteilung (Kennzahlen der Schulen), die Zuweisung von Lehrpersonen (Sozialindex, Schulniveauindex), die Kostenrückvergütung für das Untergymnasium (Herkunftsgemeinde der Schüler) oder QUIMS (Qualität in multikulturellen Schulen (Ressourcenzuweisung gemäss Fremdsprachenanteil) verwendet.

Als besonders wirksames und effizientes Mittel hat sich dabei das Web erwiesen. Dieses möchten wir neben der Distribution von Information vermehrt auch für die Erhebung der Daten nutzen – mit der Möglichkeit, die Daten online zu plausibilisieren und Personen bei der Dateneingabe direkt auf mögliche Fehler hinweisen zu können.

Den grössten Mehrwert finden wir beim Einsatz des Webs als Kommunikationsplattform. Für 2008 ist die Plattform „Schul- und Berufswahl" geplant, die die Kooperation der Schule mit der Berufsberatung fördern soll mit dem Ziel, für alle Schulabgänger eine optimale Anschlusslösung zu finden.

Seit 2006 hat der Kanton Zürich das Mandat, für den Kanton Thurgau die Bildungsstatistik zu führen. Weitere Kantone haben ihr Interesse angemeldet. Ob sich diese Ausweitung bewährt oder ob die Bista dadurch die optimale Grösse überschreitet und Flexibilität einbüsst wird die Zukunft zeigen.

Dabei bedingen sich die Ziele gegenseitig: Nur bei hoher Lieferbereitschaft, Qualität und Nutzwert werden Analysen angefordert. Häufigkeit und Vielfalt der Analysen ihrerseits bringen die notwendige Erfahrung, bringen Feedback und Einsicht in die Verwendung der Auswertungen und fördern schliesslich die Qualität.

Man kann sich natürlich fragen, ob es Ziel einer Verwaltungseinheit sein kann, die Nachfrage zu steigern. Nach unseren Erfahrungen können wir unseren Aufwand durch das Anbieten von Standard Informationen über die Website gering halten. Effektiv erheben und verarbeiten wir heute weit mehr als das Zehnfache an Information mit kürzeren Lieferzeiten und höherer Qualität zu geringeren Gesamtkosten als 1998, vor der Einführung der Individualstatistik.

Zusammenfassung und Ausblick
Die Bista Zürich versucht, aus ihren Daten möglichst vielen Interessenten möglichst grossen Nutzen zu erbringen mit der Überzeugung, dadurch die Qualität der Daten und der Analysen zu erhöhen, und mit der Hoffnung, so letztlich der Bildung zu dienen. Speziell die Verwendung der Daten für operative Aufgaben erzwingt Präzision. Verwaltungsintern werden die Daten beispielsweise für die Schulbeurteilung (Kennzahlen der Schulen), die Zuweisung von Lehrpersonen (Sozialindex, Schulniveauindex), die Kostenrückvergütung für das Untergymnasium (Herkunftsgemeinde der Schüler) oder QUIMS (Qualität in multikulturellen Schulen (Ressourcenzuweisung gemäss Fremdsprachenanteil) verwendet.

Als besonders wirksames und effizientes Mittel hat sich dabei das Web erwiesen. Dieses möchten wir neben der Distribution von Information vermehrt auch für die Erhebung der Daten nutzen – mit der Möglichkeit, die Daten online zu plausibilisieren und Personen bei der Dateneingabe direkt auf mögliche Fehler hinweisen zu können.

Den grössten Mehrwert finden wir beim Einsatz des Webs als Kommunikationsplattform. Für 2008 ist die Plattform „Schul- und Berufswahl" geplant, die die Kooperation der Schule mit der Berufsberatung fördern soll mit dem Ziel, für alle Schulabgänger eine optimale Anschlusslösung zu finden.

Seit 2006 hat der Kanton Zürich das Mandat, für den Kanton Thurgau die Bildungsstatistik zu führen. Weitere Kantone haben ihr Interesse angemeldet. Ob sich diese Ausweitung bewährt oder ob die Bista dadurch die optimale Grösse überschreitet und Flexibilität einbüsst wird die Zukunft zeigen.

Defining Data Quality for Decision Support Systems in Education

Jeffery Watson

As education moves into the twenty-first century, decision support systems are playing an increasingly critical role in decision making, planning, and program evaluation. Many U.S. districts are retooling information systems that were originally designed for reporting and accountability into systems that support the identification of *'what works'* for improvement and quality. However, using legacy data systems in new ways can quickly expose limitations. Data quality is an example of one limitation that has a profound impact on the capacity of decision support systems. This chapter briefly describes three increasingly common decision support use cases and how data quality impacts the degree to which district leaders can answer *what works* questions. Data quality is deconstructed into six dimensions that together present a framework for defining and improving data quality.

Developments in federal education policy in the U.S. are now making it imperative for districts and states to be able to attribute changes in outcomes (e.g., student achievement) to organizational units (e.g., schools, staff) and programs (e.g., professional development). No Child Left Behind (NCLB) requires U.S. schools to test all students in Grades 3 through 8 (as well as once in the high school Grades 9-12) *and* more importantly, show improvement for all subgroups, including those that have traditionally lagged behind (U.S. Department of Education, 2007). Schools in urban settings are especially challenged because they have a higher percentage of children that are harder to serve due to socioeconomic inequities, but they also often have fewer high-quality educators (Peske & Haycock, 2006). Urban districts are also facing diminishing enrollment and operating budgets, as many parents are choosing to enroll their children in private and charter schools, and consequently districts have to decide which schools to close.

Recent shifts in U.S. federal funding policy have increased the importance of program evaluation for many types of federally funded grants. Organizations that receive grants to design or implement new programs must demonstrate how they will attribute changes in performance to the implementation of the program in question. At the same time, the U.S. Department of Education (Dept. of Ed.) is funding projects that extend the design specifications of education information systems. The Longitudinal Data System (LDS) program is supporting efforts in 27 states' to create and improve longitudinal information systems with over $100 million in information technology investments. Likewise, the Teacher Incentive Fund (TIF) is awarding money to 40 local and state education agencies wanting to implement performance pay systems. These projects all have heavy information technology components because the analytics involved in determining individual pay amounts are based in part on measuring growth in student learning while controlling for prior achievement. No longer are test data associated with *just* accountability. Not only do districts and states need to know which schools are effective, but they also need to know which programs, schools, principals, and teachers are the most (and least) effective.

These new kinds of decision support efforts require copious amounts of high quality information. For example, to be able to estimate the impact of a classroom on student learning (as is the case in performance pay) it is necessary to know about the primary student – teacher relationship within each and every classroom. It may also be necessary to know about other secondary teacher – student relationships that might exist such as instructional aides, student teachers, and team teaching. Likewise, teachers receive support from building leaders in the form of mentoring and resource allocation. A rigorous attempt to attribute learning to instruction and program resources requires complex data representations of how students come into contact with teachers, school and district programs, and other significant factors (Thorn, Meyer & Gamoran, 2007).

Fortunately, recent developments in information technology are increasing districts' capacity to meet these decision support challenges. Middleware, data warehousing and reporting tools are becoming very common, if not ubiquitous in larger U.S. districts. Warehouse design has been used by large business for over a decade and has reached a fairly mature state – even reaching down into mid-sized districts and businesses. Likewise, the Schools Interoperability Framework Association (SIFA) has gained significant momentum on data specification and integration tools, and is improving the degree to which developers are able to provide districts with systems that are increasingly integrated (Schools Interoperability Framework Association, 2007). Districts are much less likely to be hampered by a lack of storage, processing cycles, or bandwidth as they once were. These factors suggest that the field of information technology in U.S. education is ripe for innovation and adoption.

It is also common that districts and schools are awash in data, yet all too often, data are collected without a sense of how it may inform changes in practice. Data collection with unclear purposes may result in stakeholders marginalizing the importance of data and perceiving information systems as a burden rather than a resource. Additionally, many districts are currently faced with the problem of knowing how to improve the quality of their data before they can meet the new decision support needs of district leaders.

Decision Support Use Cases

The goal of this chapter is to identifying the dimensions of data quality within the context of education decision support. Three use cases are briefly presented in order to provide context for the further examination of data quality. These use cases have been selected to represent the new kinds of decision facing districts (Table 1). They vary in their breadth and complexity, but together represent the new kinds of decisions education leaders are making. The most straight forward use case is that of ranking schools. Traditionally districts have used metrics such as percent of students at proficient and above to rank schools (referred to as attainment). However, many districts are beginning to use value-added analysis to compare schools based on the amount of growth on student learning. For example, one district uses both types of metrics to rank and compare schools. Schools are identified as one of four types: high attainment – high growth, high attainment – low growth, low attainment – high growth, low attainment – low growth. Generally speaking, the data required for this kind of decision support will come from just two systems; the student information system and the assessment system.

Use Case	Description	Source Systems				
		Student Inf. System	Assessment	Human Resource	Teacher Evaluation	PD* Mgmt. System
Ranking Schools	Using a combination of metrics to differentiate schools based on student outcomes.	√	√	n/a	n/a	n/a
Performance Based Pay	Determining teacher salaries in part on student achievement, teacher evaluation and creditionals.	√	√	√	√	n/a
PD* Planning and Evaluation	Using a combination of metrics to estimate the impact of professional development programs.	√	√	√	√	√

* Professional Development

Table 1: Source Systems for Decision Support Use Cases Typical of U.S. Urban Districts.

The second use case is the use of data, especially student achievement data, to drive performance-based pay systems. Many districts are basing teacher salaries on a combination of growth in student learning, teacher evaluations, and participation in professional development. As can be seen in table 1, this kind of decision support draws from more source systems. Consequently, the data issues are more complex, and there are more opportunities for problems with data quality to arise. The final use case considered here is that of evaluating the efficacy of a professional development program. Teacher professional development is considered to be the best way of improving education. However, not all professional development efforts are equal (Porter, Garet, Desimone & Birman, 2003). Efforts are underway to connect the rather large expenditures on professional development to gains in performance. Minimally, evaluating professional development requires acquiring data from a variety of sources, including the student information system, assessment, human resources, teacher evaluations, plus professional development management system.

Dimensions of Data Quality
The remainder of this chapter presents six dimensions of data quality that are key to understanding how information systems must evolve to meet the new types of decisions education leaders are facing. Individually, these dimensions represent design requirements for overhauling district data systems for the purpose in building decision support capacity. Based on work with several large U.S. districts across multiple projects, these dimensions focus attention on the functional role of data and information systems within decision making. These dimensions do not specify a data model per se, nor do they specify content (e.g., prescribes a data dictionary). The dimensions presented here compliment the work by SIF and the DQC by focusing attention on the role of data within the context of decision making and the technology environments of large districts.

Six dimensions of data quality are: accuracy, granularity, validity, interoperability, relational model, and reducibility. Each of these are defined and discussed below. Each of these are defined and discussed below.

Accuracy is the degree to which data correctly reflects reality. Are the data correct? This is a fundamental aspect of data quality, and is probably one that easily comes to mind for most people when they confront the issue of data quality. An example of poor accuracy comes from a large urban district that recently attempted to merge teacher certification data from their human resource system with teacher course assignment data from their student information system. In theory, the teachers in these two systems should match each other, but in reality, only about 80% of the records matched on name or identification number. Common causes for inaccurate data include poorly designed data entry interfaces, inadequate training, human error, and others (English, 2002).

Validity is the degree to which data measures an intended construct. Does the data, regardless of its accuracy, represent the attribute or variable that it is supposed to? In a simple example, the U.S. census bureau changed the way in which race and ethnicity are measured. Instead of coding for race and ethnicity together (e.g., White, Black, Hispanic, etc.), the bureau now codes for race and ethnicity separately, so that now it is possible to differentiate race and ethnicity independently (e.g., Black Hispanics versus Caucasian Hispanics). One common example in education is the school of record for any given student. While most students do not change schools during an academic year, many do (especially in urban settings). Thus, the school at which they are tested may not be the school at which they received most of their instruction. Hence, many districts will only hold schools accountable on those students who were enrolled for a full academic year. In both instances, the validity of reporting student achievement by school becomes increasingly invalid as the number of mobile students increases. In education information systems, we are also concerned about the degree to which tests assess what is supposed to be taught. Test validity is important especially if a district supports the use of local assessment data within the larger context of district decision support. The validity of principal and teacher evaluation data is often questioned when they are used within to determine compensation.

Granularity is the number of individuals (e.g., students), items (e.g., test questions), or length of time interval (e.g., semester versus yearly attendance) over which data are aggregated. Data quality suffers when the granularity of data do not support the analytic lens, or unit of analysis, of decision makers (Thorn, 2001). For example, in urban districts, student mobility is often cited as a problem for schools because student who are mobile are exposed disjointed instruction and curriculum. Attempts to control for the amount of time a mobile student spends between two schools requires student – school data sampled at a regular frequency. Experience however shows that student – school relationships are usually only captured at most a few times a year. Thus any attempt to control for multiple school sites on student outcomes is limited by too large grained size (i.e., under sampled) student enrollment data. The central concern when considering the *granularity* of source system is whether or not data supports a sufficient drill down (either across people, assessment measures, or time) to support the use case.

Interoperability is the degree to which data are integrated across source systems. Generally, information systems in U.S. education are not integrated, although the Schools Interoperability Framework (SIF) has made significant progress towards a establishing a unifying data model for developers. Likewise, SIF has also developed a model for web services based systems and a testing harness for zone integration servers and system agents. However, most districts do not currently have a high degree of interoperability between source systems. Data quality usually suffers when systems are not integrated for many reasons. First, when systems are not interoperable, data from one system will have to be entered by hand into another. For example, if a student information system is not integrated with the human resource system, then teacher data will have to be entered into both. Such a scenario leads to an increased likelihood of spelling and typographical errors. Also, teachers names often change when teachers get married, resulting in the need to update teacher data in two, rather than one, systems. Integration in such a scenario would involve matching records between the two systems using a combination of automated and manual methods and is likely to be expensive and difficult.

Relational is defined as the degree to which an information system's underlying data model is capable of capturing the nuance of reality. When the model is not able to store the state of affairs within a school, the quality of data about student – teacher relationships will diminish. For example, many student information systems do not capture nuanced approaches to scheduling. Most systems allow schools to enter one teacher assignment for each course. When teachers decide to team teach, or otherwise collaborate during instruction, it becomes difficult if not impossible to record teacher assignments with the student information system. Other examples of scheduling approaches that are difficult to capture include block scheduling, remediation interventions, and special education instruction because the underlying data model is not designed to do so.

Reducibility is the degree to which data supports the formation of categories of entities. For example, teachers are often labeled as math or science, or as being assigned to a particular grade. Assigning teachers as either math or science teachers when they in fact teach across content areas, would be an over reduction of teacher assignment data. Likewise, assigning students to one school when in fact they were mobile is also an over reduction of student enrollment data. Many times the causes of over reduction of data lie in how data are pulled from source systems and pushed into a repository (e.g., a data warehouse).

Application of the Data Quality Dimensions

These data quality dimensions can be systematically applied to decision support to understand data quality requirements for systems development and redesign efforts. Table 2 provides example questions that arise when the data quality dimensions are used to evaluate data quality needs of the three use cases discussed in this chapter. For example, when ranking schools, assessing accuracy will likely lead to determining whether or not student enrollment data is correct and whether or not student identifier and demographic data correct. Likewise, for performance based pay systems and professional development evaluations, it becomes important to correctly identify teacher – student linkages, teacher participation in professional development, and the degree to which disparate systems agree with one another. Answering these questions will guide stakeholders towards identifying deficits in data quality. In some cases, the questions that arise may represent a previous blind spot of stakeholders that would otherwise have gone unseen.

Defining Data Quality for Decision Support Systems in Education   107

Dimensions	Use Case		
	Ranking Schools	**Performance Based Pay**	**Professional Development Planning and Evaluation**
Accuracy	Are all schools and student groups correctly assigned to grades and schools? Are demographic data accurate?	Are student-teacher relationships in SIS correct? Do teachers in SIS match teachers in HR system?	Is data about PD participation correct? Are student-teacher relationships correct? Do teachers in PD management system match those in SIS?
Granularity	Do data support aggregation at the school level? Do data support overall-content and sub-content reporting?	Do data support using a unit of analysis that matches the performance pay systems (e.g., individual teacher bonuses)?	Do data support multidimensional aggregation? For example, using a subset of item responses to evaluate impact on student achievement when the PD is expected to only impact certain subject areas.
Validity	Do assessments measure learning? Is the validity of metrics proportional to the consequences of the measurement?	Are performance metrics consistent with other performance measures? Do student-teacher links captured in SIS reflect those in classrooms?	Do data reflect meaningful differences in PD? (e.g, Does attended hours provide a valid measure of the amount of PD content delivered?)
Interoperability	Is merging assessment files to enrollment files efficient?	Can students be connected to teachers and other instructional staff?	Can data from PD system, HR, and SIS be merged? Is the process efficient?
Relational	Do the source systems support collecting data for all students and schools?	Is SIS data model able to capture secondary student-teacher relationships?	Does SIS support connecting teachers with PD to students (including non-primary teacher-students relationships)?
Reducibility	Are special schools well represented by categories?	Are teachers being 'forced' into one particular content area? Do categories represent *all* teachers?	Can PD events be classified and sorted into types of events? (e.g., middle school math PD)

Table 2: Application of DQF to Decision Support Use Cases.

Finally, using these data quality dimensions can help guide future systems development efforts by focusing on end-use applications of data systems. Therefore, these dimensions should help improve education decision support systems both in the short and long run.

References:

English, L. (2002). The essentials of information quality management. DM Review, 12(9) 34-44

Peske, H. G., Haycock, K. & Education Trust, W., DC. (2006). Teaching inequality: How poor and minority students are shortchanged on teacher quality: A report and recommendations by the education trust . Education Trust.

Porter, A. C., Garet, M. S., Desimone, L. M. & Birman, B. F. (2003). Providing effective professional development: Lessons from the Eisenhower program. Science Educator, 12/(1), 23.

Schools Interoperability Framework Association. (2007) Schools Interoperability Framework TM Implementation Specification 2.0r1. Retrieved August 15, 2007 from http://specification.sifinfo.org/Implementation/2.0r1/

Thorn, C.A., Meyer, R.H. & Gamoran, A. (2007). Evidence and decision making in education. In Moss, P. (Ed.). Evidence and Decision Making (pp. 340-361). Malden, MA: Blackwell.

Thorn, C.A. (2001). Knowledge management for educational information systems: What is the state of the field? Education Policy Analysis Archives, 9(47). Retrieved November 2001 from http://epaa.asu.edu/epaa/v9n47/

U.S. Department of Education. (2007). Standards, Assessment, and Accountability. Retrieved August 15, 2007 from http://www.ed.gov/nclb/accountability

Data integration and school management systems in the United Kingdom

Don Passey

Introduction

The mark-book has played, over a long period of time, a significant set of roles for teachers. It has provided formative as well as summative views of attainment and achievement, views of progress when marks have been monitored in an ongoing way, and, when data has been shared with colleagues, it has offered cumulative views across year groups and through Key Stages. So, now we have access to electronic communication support systems, do we merely replace it with an electronic equivalent, or do we give teachers something significantly better, more versatile and fulfilling wider educational objectives?

If it is agreed at national or local level that providing systems to support what might be called 'curriculum intelligence' through data handling for teachers and managers is a worthy aim, then who should construct and maintain such systems, how can they be constructed and amended as new needs and ideas for use arise, and what should be included so that teachers can easily use such a system? These key questions are particularly relevant when considered within the current context of data handling practices in the United Kingdom (UK).

Why is data integration a particular challenge?

Over the past 10 or more years, data records in the UK have been more systematically undertaken electronically, the number of data holding facilities has increased, forms of data that are recorded and reported have widened, ways to handle data have diversified, and analyses and presentational facilities have become more sophisticated. For teachers this has led to an increase in available data handling facilities, offering wider analytical or 'intelligence' facility. Overall, however, it has not been easy to provide an integrated data-handling framework for teachers to access with a full understanding of its pertinent uses. The provision of facilities arising from an increasing range of commercial, national, research, local, and pilot sources has provided continuing shifts, but without integration. Different forms of provision have focused on different needs, ranging from teacher curriculum and school management needs, to national priorities, research-identified gaps, local and pilot opportunities.

School management information systems (MISs) in the UK were initially developed using information technologies (IT), created in standalone form. The IT offered functionality sufficient for limited numbers of machines in any one school, with certain individuals having rights of access. Roles of personnel who did have access were concerned largely with recording and reporting of data, rather than its analysis. Even when analyses were undertaken, this was largely seen as an administrative or management responsibility (not a direct curriculum need). Communication technology aspects were not integrally involved at those early stages, this form of functionality being developed later.

Current MISs need to be very different from those provided through standalone technologies. The two commercial companies that provide MISs for the majority of schools in the UK are Capita SIMS (Capita Children's Services, 2007), and Facility CMIS (Facility, 2005). These MISs now need to be accessible by large numbers of personnel in any one school (including all teachers), they need to function by using communication technology elements (to provide access when and as needed, and for enabling sharing of data to greater extents), and they need to provide analyses of learning outcomes and issues rather than being mere repositories of data. Policy decisions at national levels have determined the need for MISs to offer widening curriculum support, challenging providers to develop uses of standalone systems to forms that meet local and national needs using increasing communication and web-service applications.

These challenges do not fall into a simple technological group; and there is a need to consider changes at a curriculum level, as well as at a technological level. Because data handling opportunities come from a variety of sources, an integrated approach requires development to accommodate, for the end user, the range of: purpose and data origins (teachers need to know where data comes from, and the purpose of each facility); data holding (teachers need ready access, without needing to move between different data holding sites); data handling (teachers need to know how data is handled and any statistical implications); and data presentation (teachers need ease of view, to readily compare outcomes from different data handling facilities where appropriate). In the UK, data handling facilities have not generally been integrated at any of these levels, so teachers have needed to: question the purposes and possible overlap from each provider; access different data holding facilities to access different details; question the statistical validity and implications of each data facility; and question and understand presentational outcomes of each facility.

It is clear that teachers desire integration at the widest level, and there are different technological ways in which integration might be accomplished. Creating a national interoperability platform, promoted by the British Educational Communication Technology Agency, offers one approach (Becta, 2007); creating an umbrella technology to draw data at a local level into an integrating structure is an alternative (explored by START since 2000, reported in Passey, 2007, and provided commercially by Edix Live, 2007). Options can offer alternatives, but they might create diversionary pathways if, as has been shown by past experience, there is a lack of sustained management direction.

The diversification of data handling facilities in the UK
Overall, diversification of data handling facilities in the UK has been fuelled by needs identified at certain times by five different groups: commercial providers (in school MISs); national providers (with facilities to support national priorities and needs); research providers (offering alternative analyses or facilities); local providers including schools (supporting identified gaps in provision); and pilot providers (offering developments at a pilot level).

School MISs have not been provided centrally by government or government departments, but have been supplied by a number of companies and purchased by schools. These MISs have traditionally offered a great deal more functionality than that needed to support curriculum data management handling. For example, they have provided facilities to hold financial records and staff records. The sensitivity of these data has supported the view of managers taking responsible stances that such data and its handling should be isolated and restricted. Other providers have recognised that as the communication functionality of ICT systems has increased, and the potential of these facilities has been recognised and used to allow data flow and transfer of information, some sources of data and analytical approaches should be accessible more widely at a national level. The government education department (the DfES, and latterly the Dcsf) has provided, since about the year 2000, additional data management resources for schools. Initially the facilities came in CD-ROM accessible format, based on analyses of prior attainment data to generate regression statistics, offering sets of estimated likely outcomes. This system was called Pupil Achievement Tracker (PAT) (Dcsf, n.d. b). Online prior end of Key Stage attainment results became accessible to schools through the Key to Success data base (Dcsf, n.d. a). Latterly, PAT has been integrated into an online system called RAISEonline, which offers facilities in addition to regression analysis statistics and estimated likely outcomes (Ofsted and DfES, n.d.). Estimated likely outcomes generated from alternative statistical approaches have been provided by a research charity, the Fischer Family Trust (FFT, n.d.), initially to local authorities (LAs), and latterly to schools more directly.

Systems provided by both commercial suppliers and the government department have offered resources that have been used by school managers, advisers and inspectors, but reported by teachers as not always being focused for their use (Somekh et al., 2002; Kirkup, Sizmur, Sturman & Lewis, 2005). Indeed, research providers have often offered resources reported by teachers to focus on their needs. Examples include analyses of Cognitive Ability Tests (CATs) from the National Foundation for Educational Research in conjunction with the publisher NFERNelson (NFER, n.d.), and analyses of Yellis and MidYIS tests from the CEM Centre at the University of Durham (CEM Centre, 2007).

These different sources of data records and reports, whether they be government, commercial or research institution based, are held separately, without any integrated collation or presentation of data. School managers and teachers therefore need to switch between data and presentation sets in order to look across alternative analyses. The need for integration of data sources, access and links to curriculum outcomes have been recognised since at least the year 2000, but are still developing only slowly in practice. The development of new analyses and sources appears currently to be more rapid than the development of integration practices for data provision and access.

Data outcomes for teachers are being supplemented currently from sources that anayse pupil online use of out-of-school revision-style resources, such as those offered by SamLearning (SamLearning.com, n.d.) (in some respects analogous to data stored and reported through parts of the selGO initiative in schools in Germany) (selGO, n.d.). Perceived limitations in areas of data intelligence are being addressed both through local and pilot initiatives (for example, 4Matrix, n.d.), and through facilities devised by individual schools (for example, the Track to Success facilities developed by a school in Wakefield, 2007). Clearly ways to integrate these newly arising data handling facilities need to be found, if ease of access is an aim. At a technological level, Edix Live and 4Matrix have established ways to source from different data holding facilities; at a curriculum level, the Specialist Schools and Academies Trust (SSAT, 2007) have offered schools ways to triangulate analyses and presentations from different sources.

Figure 1 illustrates some of the complexity that a teacher might face when accessing a feasible array of 9 different data facilities in a school. The figure shows that the data are held in 7 separate data base sets (with links allowing ease of data transfer in only 2 cases, which means that if teachers want to integrate data from other data base sets then they need to make a transfer in some more manual way such as copying and pasting). Data are handled through online systems in 8 separate ways (so teachers need to understand the reasons and implications of these separate data handling functions if they are to use them reliably). Analyses of data are presented through 9 separate tools (2 of these are likely to be provided offline as hard copy reports, and it will be necessary to use separate individual online log on details to access the other 7 tools).

Data integration and school management systems in the UK 113

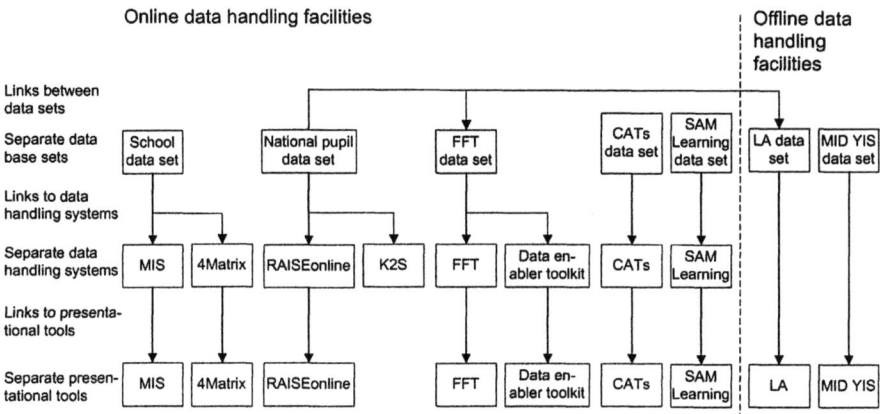

Figure 1: School access to separate data facilities and non-manual links between them

It is clear from this illustration that integration is not widely provided (when a system such as Edix Live or START are not used) in three areas: data holding (through linked data base sets); data handling (through systems showing differences in approach and implications); and data presentation (through parallel or integrated views). Integration that seeks to address just one of these elements will provide only limited integration from the user's viewpoint.

The challenges for integration
Schools and managers have often invested heavily in specific MISs, so ideally integrated systems need to work with existing MISs, integrating multiple facets of data that exist in different places. If teachers are to use integrated systems routinely and often, then those systems need to be easy to use, and aimed at the classroom teacher, as well as the form (pastoral) tutor, subject department, and school managers. If schools and teachers are to 'own' data handling systems, then those systems need to be based on facilities and features suggested by teachers and managers as supporting their needs (and allowing their individual approaches to be incorporated into them).

To support teaching and learning perspectives, integrated systems need to offer access to a range of analyses and presentations that offer curriculum views of class, form group, subject domain and year group data. Such views need to show how data analysis can be considered progressively across a school year through a series of data handling elements, with data facilities selected and used in a coherent way. To support teachers at an informational level, information and help facilities should be built into integrated systems. Email contact facilities can allow teachers to ask questions as and when desired (and with new domains encountered, many initial questions are likely to arise, so a questioning approach should itself be encouraged and managed if teachers are to engage actively).

Teachers need access to an agreed minimum data entitlement (both in terms of recording data, and in terms of gaining access to intelligence through data presentation). Teachers need access to facilities where they can enter:
- Subject targets, set at the beginning of a year or Key Stage, for each pupil in each subject. Teachers should have access to appropriate estimated likely outcomes to inform targets they set, and these might then be usefully checked by more experienced data handling users, both heads of subject departments and senior managers in schools. Across the data handling facilities outlined here, MISs, Track to Success, Edix Live and START allow teachers to enter subject targets, but in different ways.
- Subject assessments, entered on agreed occasions across the year, for behaviour, attendance, effort, and homework as well as for subject attainment. Across the data handling facilities outlined here, MISs, Edix Live and START allow teachers to enter this range of subject assessments, with Edix Live and START providing forms of data links to MISs.

In terms of presentations of analyses of data, teachers need access to lists of data on each pupil, as well as data that is collated in graphical forms by class and year group and highlights data outside normal expected ranges (called 'exception reports' by FFT). The data types to which teachers need access are:
- Background results (prior national attainment results in each subject at the end of each Key Stage, presented in forms for teachers to compare results in their subject with those in other subjects). Across the data handling facilities outlined here, Key to Success, PAT and RAISEonline, Fischer Family Trust, 4Matrix and Data enabler toolkit provide background national attainment results, while other facilities draw on some of these sources.
- Estimated likely outcomes for the end of the next Key Stage (statistically produced, with ideally a selection from the full range possible, as different estimated likely outcomes are based on different statistical calculations). Across the data handling facilities outlined here, PAT and RAISEonline, Fischer Family Trust, CATs, 4Matrix and Data enabler toolkit provide estimated likely outcomes, while Data enabler toolkit, Edix Live and START are known to show a range.
- Target summaries (so that teachers can consider similarities or differences between their subject and other subjects). Across the data handling facilities outlined here, MISs, PAT and RAISEonline, Fischer Family Trust, Track to Success, Edix Live and START provide target summaries.

Data integration and school management systems in the UK 115

- Target histories (to see the stage of the target setting process reached, and whether targets match estimated likely outcomes). Across the data handling facilities outlined here, START provides target histories.
- Teacher assessments (so that teachers can see a progression of marks in each subject, across a year, for behaviour, attendance, effort, homework and subject attainment). Across the data handling facilities outlined here, MISs, Edix Live and START show these ranges of teacher assessments.
- Monitoring displays (so that teachers can see whether attainment matches an expected progression between prior attainment and future targets). Across the data handling facilities outlined here, MISs, Track to Success, Edix Live and START provide monitoring displays, but in rather different ways.
- Added value (so that teachers can see the value added at the end of periods of time, calculated on a stated or agreed basis). Across the data handling facilities outlined here, PAT and RAISEonline, Fischer Family Trust, 4Matrix and Data enabler toolkit provide added value summaries, in different and often specific ways, while other facilities source from across this range.
- Ideas to inform classroom practice (being able to view analyses of pupil learning approaches). NFERNelson CATs, CEM Yellis and MidYIS, and SamLearning provide forms of presentations of this type.

What needs to be achieved
If systems are to provide a full range of the facilities that teachers identify as needs when they review pupil achievement through curriculum perspectives, then a range of immediate challenges have to be met. Facilities need to be developed and implemented that offer:
- Enhanced data access, so that data is accessed (or flows) from one system to another, updated as changes take place, to avoid duplication.
- Forward and backward data flows, so that updates are provided no matter where teachers enter data.
- A central repository that brings together data generated nationally in different places, so that data can be reassigned to a school; a current school or teacher could see pupil data, and then it would be reassigned to a pupil's next school or teacher (rather than being copied and transferred through other systems).
- Ideas of 'best practice' in using data to support subject achievement and improvement. There should be the means to case study examples of effective practice of data (made accessible via data systems themselves through help files incorporated into presentations and reports appropriately).
- A rapid response mechanism to newly arising ideas and data sources, so that new analyses can be incorporated rapidly into a system, so that teachers have access within limited periods of time to new ideas and facilities .
- Links between data records and pupil completed work (by ensuring that virtual learning environments have an effective MIS at their heart).

Overall, patterns of previous developments have suggested that the longer a non-integrated situation remains unresolved, the more difficult will become the challenges. Innovation needs to be supported if such challenges are to be addressed. It appears unlikely that a competitive culture can generate or embrace innovative outcomes when situations are dominated by the perceived need to maintain certain approaches; a collaborative culture appears more likely to support and embrace achievement where the need is systemic. Government agencies, commercial providers, research groups and users (schools, advisers, LAs, and national agencies) need to find ways to integrate efforts effectively.

References:

4matrix. (n.d.). 4Matrix 'Within School Variation' Toolkit. Retrieved July 13, 2007 from http://www.4matrix.org/

British Educational Communication Technology Agency. (2005). School Management Information Systems and Value for Money: A review with recommendations for addressing the sub-optimal features of the current arrangements. Coventry: Becta.

British Educational Communication Technology Agency. (2007). The Schools Interoperability Framework (SIF). Retrieved July 13, 2007 from http://industry.becta.org.uk/display.cfm?resID=28188

Capita Children's Services. (2007). SIMS - Schools Information Management System. Retrieved July 13, 2007 from http://www.capitaes.co.uk/SIMS/index.asp

CEM Centre. (2007). The CEM Centre. Retrieved July 13, 2007 from www.cemcentre.org

Department for children, schools and families. (n.d. a). Key to Success. Retrieved July 13, 2007 from https://www.keytosuccess.dfes.gov.uk/

Department for children, schools and families. (n.d. b). Pupil Achievement Tracker. Retrieved July 13, 2007 from http://www.standards.dfes.gov.uk/performance/pat/

Edix Live. (2007). Edix Live 2007 – this time it's personal. Retrieved July 13, 2007 from http://edixlive.com/

Facility. (2005). Facility CMIS. Retrieved July 13, 2007 from www.serco.com/others/facility/independent/facilityproducts/facilitycmis/index.asp

Fischer Family Trust. (n.d.). Data Analysis Project. Retrieved July 13, 2007 from http://www.fischertrust.org/

Kirkup, C., Sizmur, J., Sturman, L. & Lewis, K. (2005). Research Report No 671: Schools' Use of Data in Teaching and Learning. Nottingham: Department for Education and Skills.

National Foundation for Educational Research. (n.d.). Research Data Services. Retrieved July 13, 2007 from www.nfer.ac.uk/about-nfer/departments/research-data-services.cfm

Ofsted and Department for Education and Skills. (n.d.). Welcome to RAISEonline. Retrieved July 13, 2007 from https://www.raiseonline.org/login.aspx?ReturnUrl=%2findex.aspx

Passey, D. (2007). Technology enhancing learning: Limited data handling facilities limit educational management potential. In Tatnall, A., Okamoto, T. & Visscher, A. (Eds.). Knowledge Management for Educational Innovation. New York: Springer.

SamLearning.com. (n.d.). SamLearning.com online learning. Retrieved July 13, 2007 from http://www.samlearning.com/

selGO. (n.d.). selGO abitur-online.nrw. Retrieved July 13, 2007 from https://www.selgo.de/selgoportal/index.php

Somekh, B., Woodrow, D., Barnes, B., Triggs, P., Sutherland, R., Passey, D., Holt, H., Harrison, C., Fisher, T., Flett, A. & Joyes, G. (2002). ICT in Schools Research and Evaluation Series – No.10: NGfL Pathfinders Second Report on the roll-out of the NGfL Programme in ten Pathfinder LEAs. London: DfES and Becta.

Specialist Schools and Academies Trust. (2007). Toolkits. Retrieved July 13, 2007 from https://secure.ssatrust.org.uk/eshop/default.aspx?mcid=22&scid=34&productid=627

Track to Success. (2007). Welcome to Track to Success. Retrieved July 13, 2007 from http://www.tracktosuccess.co.uk/

East European Case: from Data to EMIS

Vainas Brazdeikis

Introduction
Lithuania has ambitious objectives for social and economic development and integration into the European Community. Strengthening the education system is critical to achieving this goal. A lot of activities have been initiated to direct Lithuanian schools in the way of development. Management of changes and monitoring of impact of these activities require relevant, reliable and timely data and information about education system. West European countries, USA and other countries worked on that for a long time, but newcomers from East countries are living in transition, so experience of these countries could be interesting on theoretical and practical level.

The aim of this article is to show what has been done in Lithuania to smoothen transition to well organized education management system. The author of this article analyzes the situation in Lithuania, theory and the reports of external consultants (Harvard graduate education school). The article describes peculiarities of the East European country, which is in transition to the new education management information system.

Structure of the article is splitted into fourth parts: assessment of the situation on data, vision on education management information system (further EMIS), implementation of EMIS vision, the results of pilot implementation.

Assessment of the situation on data in Lithuania
In historical perspective, the idea to collect data for monitoring of performance is quite old: each year official data in Paper Statistical Form from each school and municipalities has been collected by the Ministry of Education and Science (MoES). Some data was collected by the Centre of Information Technologies of Education (CITE), some copies of data are archived at municipalities and schools. In 1996 MoES announced a project for creating modern education information system called "Mokykla" ("School"). Firstly, a single database (school, student, teachers, study program, etc.) was created for two purposes: Management (for administrators) and Professional orientation (for students). But the lack of financing did not allow to complete implementation of this project.

In 2002 a paramount investment Education Improvement Project in general education has been started in Lithuania. One of the components of this project dealt with creating EMIS. The Harvard team, consultants of this component, conducted a comprehensive assessment of the data and information needs and flows in the education system that support educational management and decision making at the ministerial, county, municipal, and school levels. The assessment work focused on three areas: (1) information needs; (2) data and database structure and flow; (3) institutional capacity of managing information. The following provides a summary list of identified problems and challenges related to the data and information:

- All departments and units in the Ministry reported that they needed some key educational data, statistics, and information to operate effectively, but they don't get these data and information in a timely and reliably fashion.
- Data and statistics in hard copy and electronic form were abundant in many places in the Ministry, and IT requirement was sufficient, but an integration of multi-year data, multi-level data, and multi-source data was not in place.
- There was a lack of trust in "others" data and statistics. So, duplication of data collection and data processing in the Ministry was common. Schools felt burdened by duplicate data collection requests.
- There were multiple software applications for hosting data records in different years, at different levels, and from different sources. There were multiple data collection methods from schools: email attachment, disk transfer, and hardcopy form. These made the integration of data from various sources extremely difficult.
- There was a continuing effort to collect new data requested by different departments while they continued to collect "old data" that "was always collected" in the past. All available instruments were getting longer and more complicated. It was even known that the old data served "no real use" but was still collected year after year.
- CITE was the central agency for managing the largest educational databases that was critical to the MoES. But it had no central web portal for hosting all critical databases of multiple years, multiple levels, and multiple sources including students, teachers, facilities, exams, etc.

Analyses flows of information showed that the flows of information were in a lot of direction (Figure 1). Harvard consultants illustrated this situation as "Much Information Flow but Little Information Consumption" (Hayn Hua, 2004),

> "there are a lot of data, personnel interested in improving the current information systems, but to other hand, the current Education Management Information System is really not a system at all, but rather a set of diffuse, loosely coupled, data collection activities and independent applications and databases" (Cassidy, 2004)

East European Case: from Data to EMIS

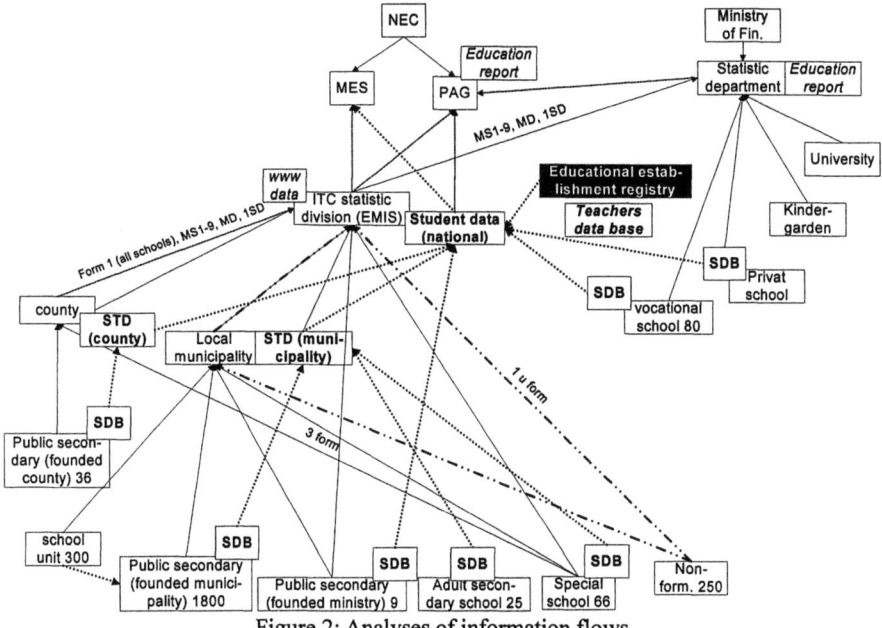

Figure 2: Analyses of information flows

So, the main problem in Lithuania was not the lack of data, but usability and balance on flows of them.

Education Improvement Project for creating new EMIS
EMIS creation in a new way was organized in 2003-2006, as a part of Education Improvement Project (further - EIP) implemented by MoES. EIP was the biggest investment project into general education schools (budget 52 million euro, 100 euro/student). The main aim of EIP was to improve educational achievements of pupils attending grades 5-10 by enhancing the quality of teaching and learning at general education schools. Objectives of this project were: (1) to enhance the quality of teaching and learning in lower secondary schools through developing professional competences of teachers, improving learning conditions at lower secondary schools, enhancing active learning of students and cooperation of teachers at schools and among schools, and *creation of a modern system of education quality management*, and (2) to optimize the utilization of education funds and resources through reduction in energy consumption in lower secondary schools and optimization of the school network. Investment into Education Quality Management System was organized through four project components: Internal & external Audit of secondary schools, Student achievement studies,

Policy analysis and Education Management information system (EMIS). All four components together with amount of funding are present in Figure 2. We could see that the biggest amount of money was allocated to creating audit system, some less to EMIS. Main goal for EMIS as a component was to provide reliable information for education managers. So, EIP allowed to start creating processes of EMIS.

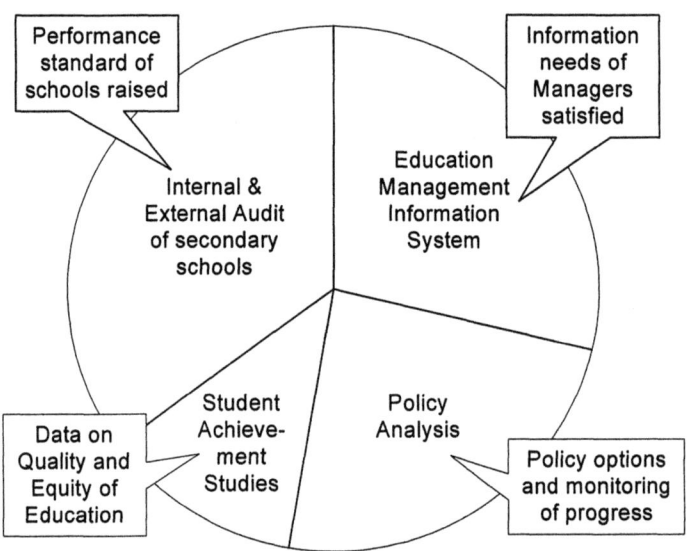

Figure 2: Education Quality components of EIP (by funding) (R. Ališauskas, 2004)

Vision of EMIS

The team of Centre of Information Technology for Education with consultants from Harvard university created a vision: EMIS is a single, stable, reliable, secure, easy-to-use centralized application and set of integrated databases and applications housed in the MES and accessed via the Internet, which all schools, municipalities, county and ministry providers and users are able to access and use with relative ease, with permissions appropriate to their level of responsibility in the system. It could be present as some structure (Figure 3) where we see suppliers of information from down and demanders of information in top. Comprehensive, Integrated EMIS data base could be as bridge builder between suppliers and demanders.

For implementation of EMIS in Lithuania regulations for EMIS as well as the project of specification for database were prepared. The regulations for EMIS provided information about target groups of EMIS, rules on how to use EMIS, information structure, names of database, etc.

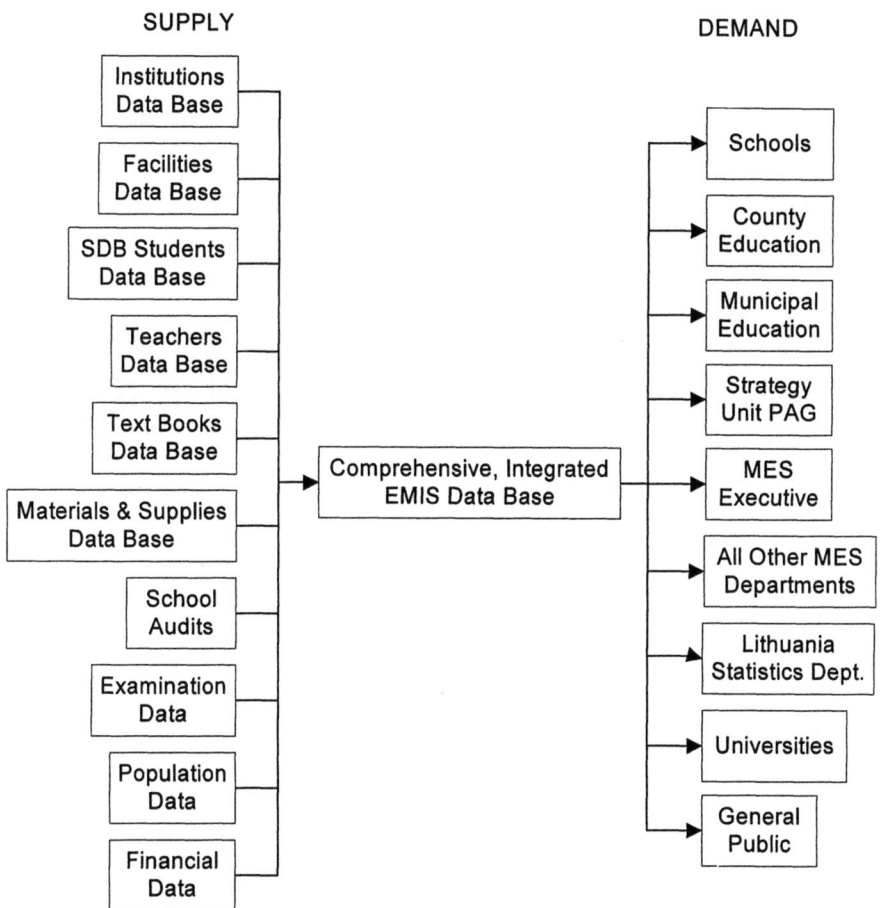

Figure 3: EMIS vision

EMIS information structure, which allows to realize new EMIS, is presented in Figure 4. On the left side we could see some database as suppliers of information (institutions, students, teachers, exams and other). The data from EMIS could be showed differentially for the deferent groups:
- For not registry users: municipalities and school profile and all levels of indicators.

- For registry users: plus data by level, years, place.
- For specific registry users (examples: researches groups, policy analyses group, Statistical department): Raw Data Tables for users.

The data from EMIS are transferring to EMIS Public data base, which allow access data through Web. EMIS Public data base are using Access&Input protocol for transferring data from different source, storage&maintenance protocol for storage data and Access&Dissemination protocol for publish data.

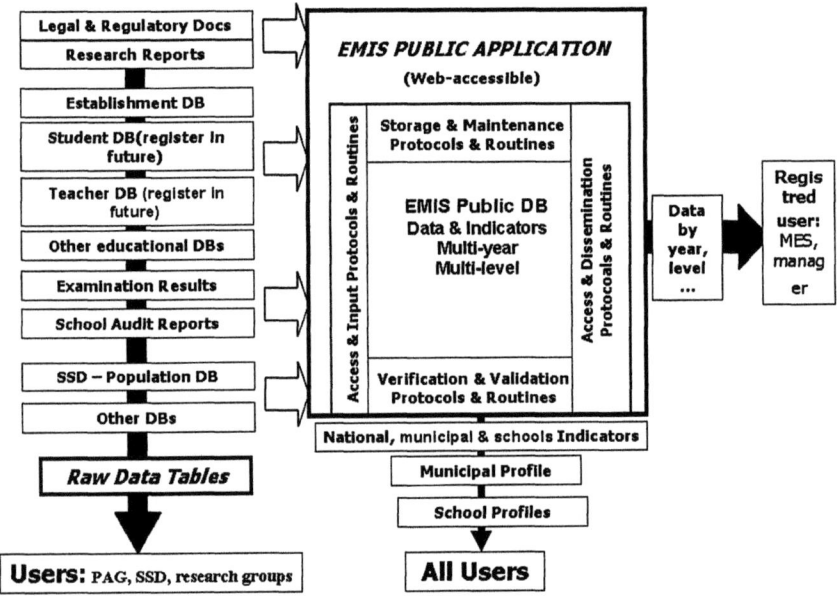

Figure 4: EMIS structure

Creators of EMIS vision agreed on some principles:
- Avoiding duplication of data (data from school must be collect from one channel and not duplicated).
- Support for schools (providing software for their own needs, computers for administration works, etc.).
- Personal data is not used.
- Feedback through reports, Web application, profiles, briefs, etc.
- Each school and municipality could organize their own MIS, but it must be integrated into national base through data exchange. Integration of data of

schools, municipalities and national level is very important: data of all levels cover each other, mainly data could be found at school level.

So, quite clear construction of EMIS was prepared, and it has provided the opportunity to work on implementation of EMIS

Implementation of EMIS

Transition to the comprehensive, integrated EMIS required a lot of activities – some that seek changes in existing organizational alignments and linkages; some that are largely technical; some related to how data is collected, processed and maintained; and some that are focused on professional development and training. All steps were planned by Three Phases as follows:
- Foundation Building.
- Development of a transitional school-based EMIS application and extensive professional development and training.
- Implementation of the new EMIS per the EMIS Vision.

In the First Phase main activities correlated with the planning process: organizational plan, human resources development, report on assessment of EMIS operation, EMIS implementation and dissemination Plans for the next cycle. The objectives were to test the overall new system design and develop capacity at the county, municipal and school levels to understand and use a new type of the system, to organize professional development and training for central EMIS staff, to develop minimum hardware standards for counties.

In the Second Phase main activities correlated with the planning initial development and testing works, integration with important external applications Development of a comprehensive, modular stand-alone school-based EMIS application, pilot test the application for internal integrity as well for user friendliness as defined by the end-users, training for county, municipal and school staff in system use Test the internet-based system, continue professional development for EMIS staff.

In the Third Phase CITE was planning to organize implementation of the internet-based System, to train county, municipal and school staff in use of the transition system, to debrief the implementation experience and plan next steps, to continue outreach to stakeholders.

EMIS Activities mainly were as:
- Data collection each year
- Data computerization of oldest data (History - 2002, 2003)
- Data integration between organizations (for example agreement with Exam centre)

- Production Data and statistical reports (national, regional, indicator)
- Data dissemination (seminar for municipalities)
- Data web site development (each year update)
- IT problem solving (computer for school)
- Staff training (Scotland, Vilnius)

Main activities of implementation were done.

EMIS Progress
As the main result of the EMIS project is EMIS website www.svis.smm.lt (http://www.svis.smm.lt/index.php?tur=8, check R1 and click on "Braižyti diagramą"). In the website you can find some sections of important information for management: data about national education indicators, municipalities and schools profiles, statistical data on table by years about students, teachers and facilities. The system allowed to create some dynamic tables. Navigation through education and regional institutions is organized through links in maps.

In final report Hua (2006) wrote that EMIS in Lithuania made a good progress:
- It had more comprehensive database than before;
- The key database is linked to key performance indicators that the Ministry of Education updated;
- It offered more convenient access for policy analysts and other education stakeholders through online as well as conventional access;
- It consolidated software application in data collection and is moving toward consolidated stage of data sharing;
- It integrated some other databases.

But some problems are still to be solved:
- Integration of data (standard for data exchange, exchange data between student e-diary and student database, data for level of general education),
- Work with users (competence of municipalities and schools staff on EMIS, recommendations for municipalities, schools on how to organize MIS (SIS), motivation (special internal), organisation and technical condition, friendly, simple system),
- Flow of information (information does not come on time, data is not completely reliable).

EMIS progress was quite well, but it still needs more input on regional level, more works on implementation phase.

Future
So, the main problem in Lithuania was not the lack of data, but usability and balance on flows of them. EIP allowed on creating processes of EMIS which helped to solve problems. A lot of activities of implementation were done in Lithuania. These activities did EMIS progress quite well, but it still needs more

input on regional level, more works on implementation phase. Experience of Lithuania could be useful for other countries and in comparative studies.

Integration of data from all levels: for standardization of data EMIS must continuously collects and integrates all educational data of MoES and must timely and reliably provide multi-year, multi-level and multi-source data to meet the needs of MoES management as well as policy research and analysis. To achieve this purpose a new project is being planned for development of staff (regional, school) competence. It is a long-term vision that municipalities in Lithuania should have capacity for educational planning and policy decisions based on data and information. This requires not only information infrastructure but also data-minded management personnel and analysts at all municipality levels. It is foreseeable that different municipalities will vary in their capacities to learn and adapt the new information-based policy management process and they will unevenly develop their capacities.

On the other hand, it is still necessary to work on the competence at national level. International cooperation and sharing experience could be organized through conferences, workshops for development of competence, joint research projects with other countries.

The European dimension could be useful to organize some university study programs on EMIS (international "credit"), to work on integration system on EU level, to invest in some software (maybe open source).

References:

All help needed here — Ališauskas, R. (2004). Development of Education Quality Management System. Presentation in the 3rd European Quality Conference for Public Administrations in Roterdame. Retrieved September 02, 2007 from http://www.mtp.smm.lt/

Cassydy, T. (2004). A Vision and a General Development Plan for a Lithuanian Education Management Information System (EMIS) (Project report). Harvard University, Graduate School of Education.

Hua, H. & Cassidy, T. (2005). Duomenys sprendimams priimti: Naujoji valdymo kultūra švietimo sistemos tobulinti. Presentation in conference in Ministry of Education and Science Lithuania. Retrieved September 02, 2007 from http://www.mtp.smm.lt/

Hua, H. (2006). Harvard Lithuania Project Report (Final project report). Harvard University, Graduate School of Education.

Ingo Jonas (Hrsg.)

Datenbanken in den Geisteswissenschaften

Frankfurt am Main, Berlin, Bern, Bruxelles, New York, Oxford, Wien, 2007.
180 S., zahlr. Abb.
ISBN 978-3-631-55719-8 · br. € 39.–*

Datenbanken in den Geisteswissenschaften werden als Arbeitsmittel, Forschungsbasis oder Archiv genutzt. Dieser Band versammelt Beiträge aus verschiedenen Disziplinen. Sie machen sichtbar, welche methodischen, forschungstheoretischen und praktischen Fragen bestehen, gilt es eine Datenbank zu entwerfen, zu pflegen, zu erhalten und/oder weiterzuentwickeln. Allen Beiträgen gemeinsam ist dabei das Interesse, das eigene Forschungsfeld weiterzuentwickeln, neue Sichtweisen zu gewinnen und/oder die Ergebnisse einem breiten interessierten Publikum anzubieten. Vorgestellt werden u. a. Datenbanken zu Spielplanauswertungen von Theatern und Forschungen zu Frauenklöstern. Im SFB 496 werden Datenbanken eingesetzt, um interdisziplinäre Untersuchungen zu ermöglichen und zu verbinden. Möglichkeiten eines polyhierarchischen Thesaurus für Designgeschichte und eines intertextuellen Zugangs zum „Kafka Bureau" bilden weitere Schwerpunkte. Eine Literaturverwaltung online und die Rezensionsdatenbank von Clio-Online, die durch Indizierung/Aggregierung entsteht, verweisen auf andere Verwendungen von Datenbanken.

Aus dem Inhalt: H. Gast/A. Mainka-Mehling: Archäologische Lebensbilder · I. Jonas: A. W. Iffland · K. Bodarwé: Female Monasticism · K. Gerlach: Berliner Klassik · S. Rüther: Rituale, Grabmäler und Schandgesten · B. Wagner/ T. Reinhard: Kafka Bureau · D. Pflugmacher: nl. Übersetzungen · K. Orchard: Kurt Schwitters Archiv · K. Albrecht: „Digitales Design Archiv" · K. Weber: Mainzer Model · A. Seidel-Grzesińska: MIDAS auf Polnisch · K. Heiligenhaus/ T. Schicketanz: Literaturmanagement · D. Burckhardt: Clio-Online: HRO · K. Lowis: BHA

Frankfurt am Main · Berlin · Bern · Bruxelles · New York · Oxford · Wien
Auslieferung: Verlag Peter Lang AG
Moosstr. 1, CH-2542 Pieterlen
Telefax 00 41 (0) 32 / 376 17 27

*inklusive der in Deutschland gültigen Mehrwertsteuer
Preisänderungen vorbehalten
Homepage http://www.peterlang.de